BLAME IT ON
BIANCA
DEL RIO

Cleanliness is NOT next to godliness. Beauty is.

BLAME IT ON BIANCA DEL RIO

The Expert on Nothing with an Opinion on Everything

BIANCA DEL RIO

3 5 7 9 10 8 6 4

Virgin Books, an imprint of Ebury Publishing.
20 Vauxhall Bridge Road
London SW1V 2SA

Virgin Books is part of the Penguin Random House group of companies whose
addresses can be found at global.penguinrandomhouse.com

Penguin
Random House
UK

First published in the United Kingdom by Virgin Books in 2018
First published in the United States by Dey Street in 2018

www.penguin.co.uk

A CIP catalogue record for this book is available from the British Library

Designed by Suet Yee Chong
Photograph on page ii © Magnus Hastings.
Photographs on pages 208 and 245 © Kevin Thomas Garcia.
All other photographs © Jovanni Jimenez-Pedraza.

ISBN 9780753553206

Printed and bound in Italy by L.E.G.O. S.p.A.

Penguin Random House is committed to a sustainable future for
our business, our readers and our planet. This book is made from
Forest Stewardship Council® certified paper.

To all of those people out there who desperately need my advice . . . but won't get it because:

  a. I'm just one woman.
  b. I'm out there trying to make a living, taping my dick to my ass and stuffing my balls in a dress so I can "entertain" people who can't entertain themselves.
  c. I don't give a fuck.

CONTENTS

AUTHOR'S NOTE

Dr. Phil is a fat, loud blowhard with a Texas twang and male-pattern baldness. I wouldn't suck his dick for a million bucks. But it turns out he's worth $400 million, and for that amount of money I'd wear his balls as earrings. I'm hitting my knees as I type.

Let's get real: the odds of my hooking up with Dr. Phil are slim and curve to the left. But the odds of my making money giving advice like Dr. Phil are pretty good. Wait; I ~~stand~~ kneel corrected: I give *better* advice than Dr. Phil. Why? Because his advice is based on education and expertise and know-how, and my advice is based on nothing but years and years of insightful prying and corrosive gossip, that's why. I don't know if I can make $400 million, but I AM something of a household name—at least in the houses of gay men, fag hags, and parents who keep wondering why their teenage son, Billy, doesn't have a girlfriend yet seems to know a lot about contouring—so I should do okay.

About a year ago, I began asking my audiences, my fans, and even my haters, all over the world, to send me questions they'd like the answers to, or problems they'd like solved. I can't *tell* you how many questions I got. I don't mean that metaphorically, I mean it literally—I'm really, really bad at math, and my loyal ~~serf~~ assistant, Jamie, is equally useless at the "counting thing." What I do know is that I've gotten enough letters to write a book. Or two. Or three. Depending on whether or not you tell your friends, families, and fuckbuddies to buy this book, so it will turn a nifty profit, and my publisher will say, "My God! Fuck Dr. Phil. *Blame It on Bianca Del Rio* is a literary gold mine. WE MUST, MUST, MUST HAVE A SEQUEL!!!"

ANOTHER AUTHOR'S NOTE

I know it's not "proper editorial form" (whatever the fuck that is) to have a second Author's Note, but I was having cocktails when I wrote the first one and left this out. So . . .

I received six billion trillion letters, emails, and FB posts from people asking me for advice. (If that sounds like a lot, I assure you it's true; Donald Trump told me that he heard this from people who told him that they read it somewhere.)

Needless to say, a lot of the questions I was asked were somewhat alike in nature, tone, and language. So when you're reading this hilarious book and think to yourself, "OMG, that's MY letter!"—it's not. Also, I've changed a lot of the names—not to "protect the innocent" but to protect me from the crazy bitches who will call and write and email over and over and over, saying, "Oh, Bianca, thank you so much for using MY letter; I knew you liked me!" Bitch, I didn't use YOUR letter; you just think I did, because you're a narcissist in desperate need of counseling or medication . . . in which case, don't forget to share.

I also got lots of emails and letters saying, "I read a question just like that in Dear Abby," which tells me two things: 1. You're old; Dear Abby's been dead for years, and 2. You need counseling; no healthy, sane person remembers random advice questions years later. Get some help.

FYI, there are A LOT of advice columnists all over the world (check out Ask Svetlana; that Siberian husky makes me howl, especially when she gives advice on diet and exercise. Poor thing's never been inside the Kremlin—because she can't fit. Also Abby, Ann Landers, Amy, the snotty queen in the Sunday *New York Times*, and my uncle Nunzio, who has both an opinion on everything and a cleft palate. He doesn't so much give advice as test your patience), and most of the questions we receive are similar. They're usually about romance ("I'm in love with a werewolf"), sex ("My werewolf boyfriend cums too quick"), money ("I think my caregiver is stealing my Medicare benefits"), or family ("My relatives are nice to my brother's kids but not mine; do you think it's because they're part werewolf?"). So don't be shocked if some of the questions feel familiar; with the possible exceptions of me and Edward James Olmos's dermatologist, everyone in the world has the same fucking problems. So get over yourselves; you're not unique—in fact, you're probably a tad boring. And, like everything else, I say that in a kind, loving way.

Oh, it's also entirely possible I just made this shit up. Love you all sooooo much! Muah.

Anyway, before I get into the meat and potatoes of the book—your needy questions and my bitter, unqualified responses—I want to thank everyone who wrote in with questions. Without you, I'm nothing. (Okay, that's not true. Without you, I'm still fabulous and my career is still on the way up, up, up! What is true is that without you, it would have been much harder for ~~Jamie~~ ME to write this book.) So thank you for taking the time to share details from your ~~pathetic~~ personal lives with me—and the world.

Shocking! Appalling! Horrifying! Her bags don't MATCH!

Early to bed and early to rise makes a man healthy, wealthy, and wise.

BENJAMIN FRANKLIN

Early to bed and early to rise makes a man ready for hospice care.

BIANCA DEL RIO

CHAPTER 1

I FOUND A LUMP

He said, "Open wide."
Old habits die hard.

I'm not a doctor, nor do I play one on TV. In fact, other than the fact that I once blew an OB-GYN in a parking lot, I have no connections to health and well-being whatsoever. Yes, I go to a gym, and yes, I work out, but not for health reasons. I have to squeeze my ass and balls into a size-six muumuu, I can't afford to gain weight or it'll cost me a fortune at Lane Bryant. I received quite a few questions on this subject, including a half-written letter from an anorexic, who ran out of energy and died when she tried to conjugate the verb *purge*.

Bianca:

Being disabled and having a hearing and sight impairment, I find it so difficult in nightclub settings to see my absolute favourite queens which include you. What advice could you give me to make it easier for people like me to enjoy a gig or event? I always find it hard to ask event organisers for help because I don't know what help to ask for. When I went to your event in Belfast I got VIP tickets in the third row but it was so hard to see you and lip read. I wish I could enjoy the full experience like a "normal person." Any advice would be appreciated.

Love you always and forever.
Danielle

Dear Danielle:

So, you're disabled, half deaf, AND half blind? Why not add cradle cap and spina bifida to the mix? How 'bout tuberculosis or shingles? Maybe you could get a job as the Elephant Man's girlfriend? I don't mean to be callous, Danielle, but I think easy-access entertainment is the least of your problems. BUT, I do have a solution for you! Have a celebrity (other than me—I'm waaaaay too busy—and cripples annoy me ☺) hold a telethon for you on TV. (Look how great it worked out for comedian/scumbag Jerry Lewis!) You'll be onstage, on camera as the poster child/sidekick for the entire time. If you do well (look the wrong way, drool on cue, strain to hear the band, etc.), you could become not only the poster child for ALL TV telethons, you could turn out to be the face of disease in Europe. Think of the endorsement deals, the public service ads, the promotional tours!!! You'll be so busy you won't have time to be wheeled in and out of drag shows!

Good luck, Danielle; time to get the ball rolling. So have some undercooked shellfish for lunch and go outside in the rain without a hat. ☺

Dear Bianca,

I am an 18-year-old lesbian. I have been out as a lesbian for the last five years, however I have recently developed a bit of a crush on a woman who is technically a man. She's a drag queen. Am I straight or bi or gay or what?

Irene
London, UK

Dear Irene,

Irene, forgive me; I'm American and you're English, so there may be a language barrier. What you are is fucked. No, really fucked. Even I'm confused by your situation. I've heard this story a thousand times . . . usually from a relative/prisoner, so your question is bothering me a bit . . . hey, wait a minute! Dad? You were worried no one was going to write in. Thanks for your support. FYI, count me in for the next conjugal visit. ♥

———————————

Dear Bianca,

After six months of dating, my boyfriend Tim and I finally slept together. He now says he wants to break up because my vagina smells awful. (I'd only slept with one boy before Tim and he said the same thing.) I don't know what to do. I'm clean—I shower, bathe, douche . . . all the things I can to stay fresh. I don't have any infections or anything. Any advice? I'm only twenty—is this going to be an issue for the rest of my life?

Jenny
Sante Fe, New Mexico

Dear Stinky,

I'm so sorry you have funky junky. Nothing kills the mood like having to whisper sweet nothings through a hazmat mask. (No matter how many times I ask, it's not kinky.) Although I haven't spent much time in Cooz County, I've done some research in an effort to help you. (And by research, I mean I tied my assistant, Jamie, to the computer, and said, "Google vajayjay!")

Turns out, a stinky snatch is not all that uncommon, and some women are simply cursed with a garden of garbage. A hetero friend of mine (yes, I have some . . . one) once went out with a beautiful, sexy fashion model. On a scale of one to ten, she was a twelve (like me). Unfortunately, her vagina made him call 911 . . . OUT THE WINDOW. He said that the moment she took off her panties, a noxious smell enveloped the room and he started having flashbacks to his days getting napalmed in Nam. In less time than it takes to say, "What died in your vag?" his evening went from foxy to foxhole. And as gorgeous as she was, and as nice as she was, he couldn't go out with her again. He said, "I'd rather stick my dick in Betty White." I said, "What about Barry White?" He said, "Him too." I said, "I agree! You know that famous saying, 'Once you go black, you lose your jewelry.'"

So, what to do about your putrid puss? I don't know if you can completely kill the smell, but I have a couple of ideas that might minimize the musk and maybe save your relationship.

1. Instead of perfume, put dog shit behind your ears and on your wrists. It'll smell so bad Tim will happily go south for a refreshing trip into Crusty Canyon.
2. Reassure him that it's perfectly safe for him to have sex with you. Before you coax/plead/beg him to put his fingers, face, or phallus into your she-cave, send in a canary first . . . and wait for the bird or a Chilean miner to return. One will tell you the conditions down there.
3. Attach a Stick Up Air Freshener deep inside one of your vaginal walls. Unless you're dating an Asian man, in which case an inch or two ought to suffice.
4. Learn to swallow; you'll be able to keep your pants on.
5. Fuck the homeless. They won't mind, you'll just have to find a place for the shopping cart.

Muah!

Hi Bianca,

I have a disease that causes me to have no hair on my head. Growing up female with no hair is a fuckery. I wear shitty wigs and hair pieces but they are super expensive if you want them to look good, which I do because I just want to blend in or even look good with my hair. But I can't afford Beyoncé hair.

Do you have any everyday-wear hair that you would suggest? Or advice on lace fronts?

Thanks,
Chrissy V

Chrissy,

When I started reading your letter, I thought, "Oh, great, another cancer victim looking for help. Bor-ring!" The cunty part of me wants to say, "If you won't tell me what disease you have then I won't give you any advice." But I'm in a giving mood today (drunk), so here goes...

Milk the bald thing for all it's worth. It's very chic, especially among the fashion, style, and artsy types. If you wear dramatic earrings, people will think it's a look, not a disability. (I hope your disease doesn't prevent you from having the strength to put on the earrings.) Plus, you'll save a fortune on wigs, glue, tape, shampoo, and conditioner. And if people DO think you have cancer, milk that, too. Cut the lines, take the good parking spots, be the first one in the triage tent during a disaster. And finally, when you're giving your boyfriend head, all you have to worry about is getting it in your eyes! (Unless your secret disease has taken your eyes, too, in which case, tattoo a bull's-eye between your boobs, and yell, "Fire away" when he gets close.)

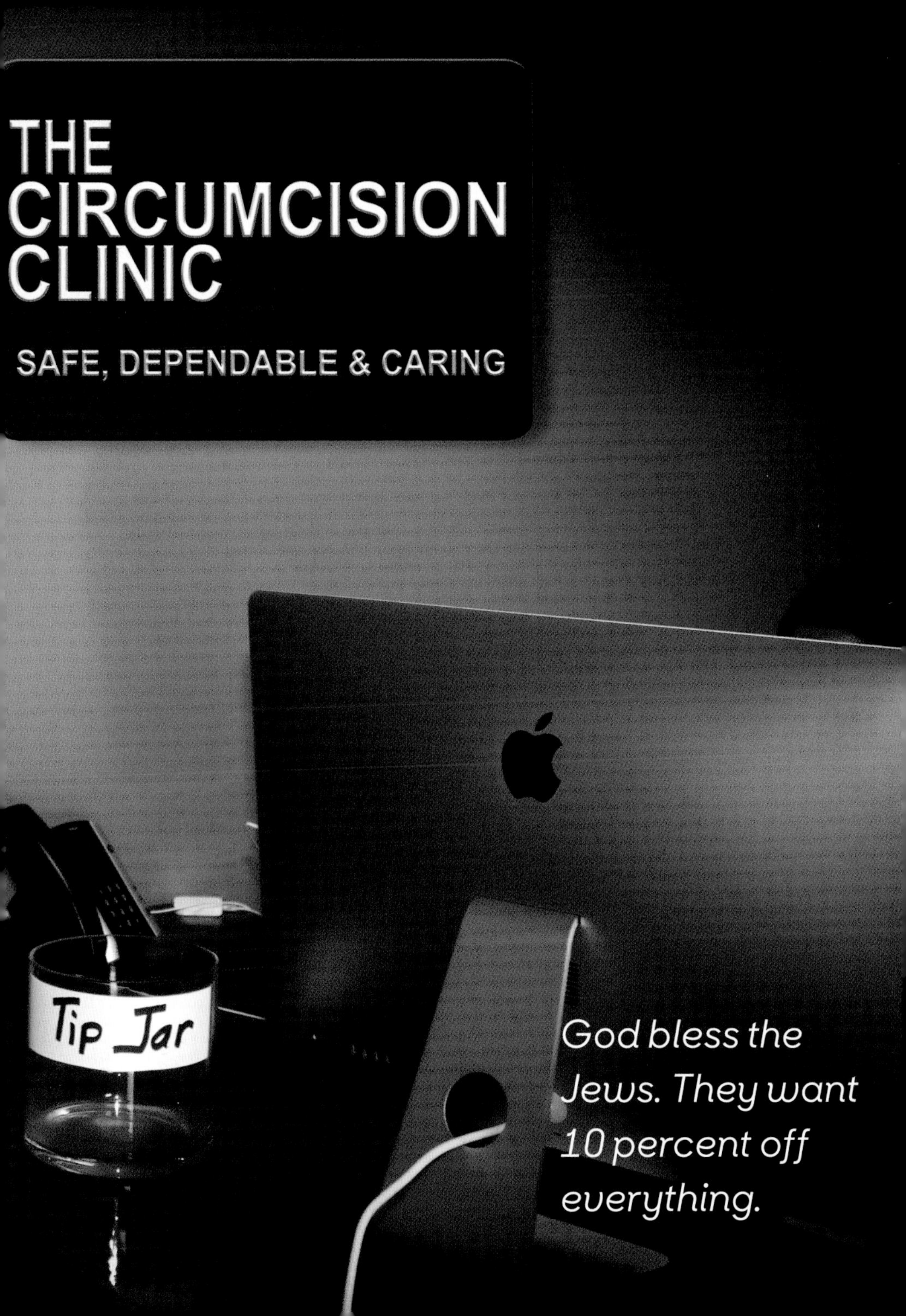

God bless the Jews. They want 10 percent off everything.

Dear Bianca,

We have three children, as do our neighbors, who we like quite a bit. The issue is that our neighbors are very heavy and their children are becoming morbidly obese. We don't want our children going over to their house for dinner, because we know they will not eat healthily. We're also worried about their children's health. Can we say or do anything?

Donna & James
Midland, Texas

Dear D&J,

Aren't fat people fun? There's no end to the problems they have! First thing to remember is that the tubby trio are not YOUR children, and while they're disgusting to look at, and probably won't live past thirty, they're not your responsibility. If Massive Mommy and Dirigible Daddy don't see a problem with their obese offspring, why should you? (I'm guessing they don't see the problem because they can't see them over the piles of potato chips and pizza boxes on the table.)

I think it's perfectly fine to let your children go over to their house to play—either before or after dinner, not during. Although I'm guessing that even snack time might be a challenge, and could involve fifty loaves of bread and a Guernsey cow.

Saying something to Mr. & Mrs. Fatass might ruin a friendship, so I suggest you let go of your ~~revulsion~~ concern, and make their hideous appearances work for you! Spend time with them in public. Go to the beach, the swim club, or all-you-can-eat buffets. Wear slim-fit clothing and dark colors, and stand as close to them as you can. As passersby call 911 to arrange for "preemptive strikes," your family will look truly fabulous. And isn't that what really matters? Let's be real here.

Dear Bianca,

I had acne when I was a teenager, and it has left me with pockmarks and scars. I'm starting college in the fall and I'm afraid boys won't go out with me because of my skin. (It's not awful, just noticeable.) I find you'd know more about concealment than anyone. ☺ Any suggestions?

> *Sandie*
> *Batavia, New York*

Hey, Crater Face,

What's up? How bad are your craters? Did Neil Armstrong plant a flag on your chin and say, "One small step for man . . . "? There are a few things you can do to conceal the scars. I'm assuming you can't afford dermabrasion, or you would have done it already. So let's go the more conventional route. (And by *conventional* I mean "Instagram filters.") Try foundation and base and use so much you have to put it on with a trowel. (As long as it doesn't rain and you don't sweat, you'll be fine.) If you want something slightly more permanent, try spackle or bathtub grout. They're not as firm as makeup, but they're waterproof.

But the long-term solution has nothing to do with makeup or skin treatment. It has to do with perspective. Forget "fixing yourself" so you can get a cute guy. Just lower your standards and go out with ugly or disfigured boys. I'll bet there are plenty of burn victims who would LOVE to toss you a hump! So embrace your face and head on down to the Hospital for Reconstructive Surgery! The other option is a veil . . . made of lead.

Xoxo

———

Dear Bianca,

I recently found out I can no longer rely on Depend undergarments for an undisclosed reason. Can you recommend an alternative?

JPW
Dallas, Texas

Dear JPW,

Undisclosed reason? Seriously? How many options could there be? The problem is either brown or yellow (or gray, if you have liver issues). The alternative to Depends is staying home. If you need company, bring in someone who has a diaper fetish, and let the fun begin.

BDR

P.S. Does "JPW" stand for Just Plain Wet?

———

Bianca:

My wife Helen and I have been married for fifty-one years. She's five years older than I am and her health is starting to fail. It seems as though I'm going to outlive her. How can I prepare myself for that?

Arnold
Hallandale, Florida

Arnold,

I'm sorry to hear about Helen, but we all die. (I died last Tuesday night in Oklahoma City. Audience full of old, white Christians. It was a horror. Daniel had a better time in the lions' den.)

Since there's no way to prepare yourself for the loss of your wife of fifty-one years (especially if she liked anal), why not prepare HER? Let Helen prepare for the upcoming event; after all, she's the one heading down the tracks. Simple, unspoken acts of kindness might ease her into a gentle good-bye. For example, when she gets in bed at night shine a flashlight on her face and say, "Follow the light, Helen, follow the white light!" (I don't want to sound racist ... Black Lights Matter. Happy now, Leroy?) When she's sleeping put pennies on her eyes. In the bedroom corner, replace the crutches she leaves standing there with a shovel. "Accidentally" mix up her orange juice with formaldehyde. Maybe buy her an expensive silk nightgown, and when you take the tag off, tie it around her toe? FYI, take off the sales sticker so she doesn't feel cheap in her final hours. Little things matter. And finally, whisper sweet nothings into her good ear, things like, "You'll always be my girl, Helen," or "I will love you forever and always," or "Don't worry about me. I'll be fine. I've been fucking your caregiver since July so she can become a citizen before they build that fucking wall."

I hope that helps. Muah!

———

Bianca,

Hello! I recently underwent surgery for colon cancer & am currently on chemotherapy. I'm doing great, but not feeling very sexy at the moment. You always look fab in and out of drag, so any suggestions to make myself feel a bit more desirable?

Love you!
Rebecca
Atlanta, Georgia

I feel like Anderson Cooper on New Year's Eve— waiting for the ball to drop.

Dear Rebecca,

Sorry you're going through such a tough time; allow me to make it better!

Here are a few things to pretty up your look, lift your spirits, and help your sex life (as you know, I'm dealing with a terminal disease as well; it's called ugly):

* If you've lost your hair, get a tattoo on your head. Something like, "Not too sick to suck."
* If you have chunks of hair, dye each of them a different color and be the Rainbow Coalition of people with three weeks to live.
* Get a Louis Vuitton colostomy bag. Dress for Success!
* Write a diet book: *Eat Anything and Waste Away!*
* Write a fashion blog. You can call it *Jaundice Is the New Black.*
* Bedazzle your catheter.
* Wear a push-up hospital gown.
* Start your own fashion line: "My Mom Went to Sloan-Kettering and All I Got Was This Lousy T-shirt."

———

Bianca:

My boyfriend and I moved in together a few months ago. I have a nine-year-old daughter who lives with us. Yesterday I was cleaning and I came upon a couple of prescription pill bottles my boyfriend had in his desk drawers. They're very strong mind/mood-altering drugs. I don't know what to do.

Mimi
Miami, Florida

Dear Mimi from Miami,

I LOVELOVELOVE that you're Mimi from Miami. A human anagram! Just think, if you drive from Miami to Tampa, you'll be Mimi from Miami on the Tamiami Trail. Sounds like a new Carrie Underwood song, no? (I think I see music royalties in my future. *Ka-ching!*) I'm only talking about your name because it's funnier than your actual story.

Seriously, Mimi, there are a couple of issues here, but only one solution. Either the boyfriend, the daughter, or the pills have to go. Considering that the daughter is in your will, and the boyfriend is in your vagina, you need to get rid of the pills. Immediately!

My address is:

Bianca Del Rio

PO Box 6969

Sissyville, USA

Bianca:

My husband's brother Bill died last month after a long battle with smallpox. My husband wants to bury his remains in our garden. I'm uncomfortable with this; not just for health reasons, but the thought of having someone's remains buried in our yard feels icky. Any suggestions?

Andrea

Denver, Colorado

Dear Andrea,

Who the fuck gets smallpox anymore? What is this, 1927? (I was around then.) Was the brother a filthy pig? (I had one of those, too.) Oh, wait, that was unkind. (I'm a little tense at the moment. I'm watching teen *Jeopardy!* and the fat kid from Omaha just missed a question a retard could answer.) Allow me to rephrase: So sorry for your loss, I guess. I'm BUSY, Andrea.

I'm scribbling this like a doctor writing a prescription: I doubt you can catch anything from an incinerated Bag of Bill. Many people keep the ashes of loved ones inside their homes, on the mantel or on a shelf in the office. I have one friend who keeps his mom's ashes right on the dining room table—because sometimes salt just isn't enough. (She was fat; it would take two hands to toss her over your shoulder for luck.)

Anyhoo, the yard thing does feel a little creepy—I mean, what if the gardeners accidentally mow the poor thing into mulch, or the dog digs him up and drops him at your feet, like a squirrel he's killed? Do you say, "Good boy, Bingo," or vomit all over the dog and the deceased?

If your husband is insistent on having his brother in the backyard, then make sure that (a) he buries him in an airtight, sniff-proof container, (b) buries him VERY deep in the ground, (c) doesn't tell you where in the yard he is, and (d) never has the neighborhood kids over for a scavenger hunt . . . And no, I've never seen *Forensic Files*.

FYI, things could be worse. You may have issues with your husband burying his pox-riddled brother's ashes under your pansies, but Mrs. John Wayne Gacy had to deal with her husband burying thirty-three teenage tricks under the dining room. So, Andrea, be grateful. Put a smile on your weather-beaten face and tiptoe through the tulips! . . . And remember, moisturize. The body. Before it's in the ground. If not, it smells.

Dear Bianca,

I am in my first year of recovery from alcoholism (along with addictions to meth, cocaine, Xanax, Valium, Ecstasy, and whatever other party drugs I could get my hands on) and living in a treatment house. My AA sponsor, Brian D, makes me write a gratitude list first thing every morning, when I get up. He says I need to start each day by thanking God for all of the blessings in my life. I understand the need to be grateful but I'm not religious and don't know if I believe in God. Any suggestions?

Michael
Palm Springs, California

Dear Michael,

Your question is so complex, and so multifaceted, I don't know where to begin. I think I need a drink before I start. Gimme a sec; I'll be right back.

Okay, I'm back, Susan, thannnks for way-ting. —Oh, I'm sorry, MICHAEL. Must be the vodka talking.

For starters, your sponsor, Brian D? Is the *D* for "douchebag"? No decent person would make you write lists the MOMENT you wake up. What happened to having coffee or taking a shit, not to mention apologizing to your trick for the rash before you give him bus fare? I can think of at least twenty things to do when you get up first thing in the morning—six of them starting with the letter *F*—and none of them involve writing a gratitude list.

Ever watch the *Today* show? (I don't—I don't care about the news—but for our purposes let's pretend I do.) Do you think the first thing Hoda Kotb does when she wakes up at three o'clock in the morning is write God a gratitude list? No, of course not. Hoda pulls a fifty out of her bra to give to the makeup guy at NBC, who will cover some of the bags under her eyes and bathe her in foundation so she looks like she's under seventy. I don't mean to dis Brian D, but if he REALLY cared about your recovery, he'd let you sleep in, pretty up, and laze your way into gratitude over waffles, mimosas, and porn.

Before I continue, let me apologize for this EXHAUSTINGLY LONG answer, but your question really pushed some buttons for me; not sure why. (Can you believe I apologized for something? Neither can I!) Anyway, short-form answer to your question: Move out of the treatment center and have a fucking cocktail. We're all going to die eventually, so you might as well go out with a buzz. And now I'M going to have a few cocktails; responding to your complicated question has sucked the life out of me.

I'm back! Both Jack Daniel's and I thank you for waiting. So, gratitude? Waaaay overrated, in much the same way as getting a blow job from someone with no teeth. Oh sure, on the surface it's all dirty and fun, but when you look at the facts in front of you it ain't that hot. Yeah, the sucking is good—I've never heard anyone say, "You know, that sloppy bitch kept dragging her gums," but the reality is, you're getting a blow job from SOMEONE WITH NO TEETH. And there's a REASON that your cum dump has no teeth. And that reason is usually (a) he/she's so old she considers a catheter an accessory; (b) he/she's bulimic and her fangs rotted from daily purgings; or (c) he/she lost them to Josef Mengele in a bizarre, twin-centric, Nazi medical experiment. If the reason isn't (c) you've made a horrible choice. C is acceptable due to your "service provider's" tragic backstory. Because no matter what drama you have going on in your life, Gummo has been through worse. I don't care if you have a two-inch dick and a ball sac you could trip over, on a scale of one-to-Auschwitz, you're barely a five.

You know who ruined gratitude for me? Jesus freaks, that's who.

Next comes
waterboarding.
My advice: I don't
care how hot he is,
NEVER date a guy
who's in ISIS.

Those joyful souls are waaaay too grateful for my liking. I'm not talking about your everyday, garden-variety Christians, who are exhausting in their own special ways, but Jesus freaks. You've seen them—they wander the streets wearing crosses around their necks that are so big it would be easier for them to just strap Jesus to their back, like a carry-on or a tote. And they're always happy, happy, happy, smiling like a retarded forty-year-old man-child clapping his hands in a candy store.

Or perhaps you'd recognize them because they mention **HIS** name every five minutes, regardless of the circumstance, occasion, or context of the conversation going on. Let's say, for example, it's a simple, wholesome breakfast at Denny's.* Here's the scenario:

> **WAITRESS:** Can I start you off with a drink?
> **JESUS FREAK:** Yes. I'd like a huge, teeming glass of water . . . which I can drink today, only because Jesus the Almighty has brought the rains down from the heavens to quench the earth so that the believers and repenters can satisfy their thirst and continue to spread the word of the Lord.
> **WAITRESS:** Okay. Water it is.

Had I been that waitress, the conversation would have gone differently.

> **WAITRESS:** Can I start you off with a drink?
> **JESUS FREAK:** Yes. I'd like a huge, teeming glass of water . . . which I can drink today, only because Jesus the Almighty has brought the rains down from the heavens to quench the earth so that the believers and repenters can satisfy their thirst and continue to spread the word of the Lord.
> **WAITRESS:** We're in California. There's a drought, you asshole.

You'll get half a cup. And on your way out maybe you can ask Jesus why the fuck it hasn't rained here in five years. This place is drier than Betty White's pussy.

But it's not just the pasty, old white trash that frequent Denny's who are Jesus freaks; old black women are very fond of him, too. I was watching the news recently, shortly after one of America's weekly white-cop-shoots-unarmed-black-man-for-no-apparent-reason events. The entire family of the deceased black man was holding a press conference, and while the family attorney was at the microphone speaking, next to him, a woman (Grandmother? Great-grandmother? Aunt who raised the victim as her own child because the baby-mama was a teenage crack whore?) kept chanting, over and over, "Thank you, Jesus; thank you, Jesus; thank you, Jesus." And I'm thinking, for what? Not only was your son/grandson/nephew just killed, but you're making a fool of yourself interrupting your pro bono attorney who is announcing a multimillion-dollar lawsuit. Unless of course you're thanking Jesus for the windfall awaiting you, or for the national TV exposure that might land you a series on BET or Bravo! In which case, I stand corrected.

I, too, have no idea if there is a God or not. Maybe yes, maybe no. What I do know is that if I'm on my knees, I won't be able to thank God because my mouth will be full.

I'm taking a risk here, Michael, because I don't know if you have any immediate family members who are regulars on the charity circuit, but . . . I find the families of the genetically disabled are also overly grateful to God for the "blessing" of having a thirty-seven-year-old brother who wears a helmet to take a bath and likes to make "pies" out of his poops. I'm always wondering, what's the blessing, exactly? They've learned that shit is a therapeutic tool, and not just a couple of brown logs floating in a toilet? If they want to be grateful I think the gratitude comes in the fact that Billy's being "differently abled" gives them perfectly legitimate reasons to turn to alcohol and drugs as both a coping mechanism and a food group.

Which brings me back to you. You're living in a treatment center/recovery house—what a terrible place to get sober. You're surrounded by sober alcoholics—people for whom *everything* is a "trigger" to drink. A simple lunch at Olive Garden sounds like this: "Does the wine burn out of the chicken Marsala? Is there rum in the rum cake? Can you make a virgin piña colada?" It's less harrowing being alone in a hotel room with Bill Cosby than trying to have a snack with a recovering drunk.

I have a cousin, Barry K, who hasn't had a drink in years (which is why I haven't seen him in years), but on the occasions when we speak (usually after the unexpected death of someone we both either loved or hated), he starts every conversation by announcing that he's a "grateful recovering alcoholic." And when we hang up, my first thought is always, what the fuck is *he* grateful for? He spent years losing jobs, puking in public, and peeing himself in restaurants, and now he spends every waking moment in church basements listening to other people with no lives share about their "recovery." If I was Barry K, I wouldn't be grateful, I'd be quiet.

The last time I saw Barry, I was walking into Forgotten Woman to buy a casual top (36 Husky) and he was coming out of—guess where—a church basement. I made the mistake of saying, "Barry, how are you?" He said—guess what—"Grateful." I said, "Why??? Your shoes don't go with your pants, your fly's open, and you have coffee on your tie." He said, "I'm grateful to be sober." I said, "You'd be better off drunk. At least it would explain your look." He smiled and walked away. I smiled and walked into Forgotten Woman. And *I* was grateful that even though I'd had cocktails for breakfast I could still match a simple summer shift with an open-toed wedge.

*P.S. I don't actually eat at Denny's. Just like my handsome twenty-eight-year-old Peruvian gardener, Ronaldo, it's beneath me. I chose Denny's as a reference so I would seem more like an everyday person, and therefore make the story more accessible to the reader.

Dear Bianca:

I've been trying to lose weight, and keep it off, for years, with varying degrees of success. I've tried Jenny Craig, Weight Watchers, Deal-A-Meal. You name it, I've tried it. I belong to three different gyms, I've worked with a trainer; I'm even seeing a psychiatrist, yet nothing helps; I don't know what to do. I'm beside myself.

> *Janice*
> *Pittsburgh, Pennsylvania*

Janice,

Of course you're beside yourself—you weigh five hundred pounds. You're beside everybody. You're two people. Actually, three people, if they're all frail, petite, or in ill health with Stage Four Something or Other. Being morbidly obese is much different from just being fat. Anyone can get fat; morbid obesity takes work and requires drive and determination. Good for you! Be proud of your stick-to-it-iveness; you've made a concerted, diligent effort to become a sideshow attraction, and all of your hard work has paid off. In fact, why not BE a sideshow attraction? Why not join a circus or a carnival,

"Liza, Lorna,
don't wake Mommy.
She's just napping."

and let your massivity work for you? Monetize your girth. You can sit on a stool in a cage, half nude, and let people throw peanuts or coins or dollar bills at you while you chow down on a couple of po' boys or a small horse. *Ka-ching!*

I say, Janice, why stop at five hundred pounds; why not go to six or seven hundred, assuming your heart, bed, and reinforced Dodge Ram can handle it? Then you can start a career in television!

One of my favorite shows on TV is *My 600-lb Life*, on TLC. Janice, if you haven't seen it, put down that vat of Chunky Monkey and run—I mean lumber—into the family room and turn on the television. It's a fabulous show. It's about an Armenian doctor (whose name no one can pronounce) in Houston who does gastric bypass surgery on grotesque fat slobs—oh, I'm sorry, my bad—I mean unfortunate people dealing with weight issues. The patients have to be AT LEAST six hundred pounds to be cast on the show. It also helps if they live in a trailer and have crucifixes on the walls and lots of children bringing them food.

So, stop killing yourself trying to lose all that weight; embrace your obesity and have fun killing yourself with Big Macs! Go out and gain the other hundred pounds necessary to be one of Dr. Whatshisname's patients. Janice, you don't need to make a call for help, you need to make a call for seconds. And thirds! And when you get close to the magic number of six hundred pounds, call me . . . and I'll call the casting director at TLC! Good luck, and bon appétit!

BIANCA CHEWING THE FAT

My fascination with fatties began in 1991 when I was just a DQIT (Drag Queen in Training). I remember watching TV one night, snuggled up on the couch with my court-appointed guardian, when the nightly news came on. The lead story was about the death of a twelve-hundred-pound man named Walter Hudson from West Hempstead, New York. Shockingly (!), Walter had a heart attack and died at the age of forty-seven. And he was so fat that a local fire rescue squad had to cut a hole in the side of his house and pull him out with a forklift. I was so shocked by the spectacle of Walter's body being pulled out of the house (like a dead orca being removed from its tank at Sea World) that I vowed, with God as my witness, that even if I crammed myself into a size-two evening gown or summer shift, I would NEVER, ever eat so much that a SWAT team had to unzip me.

I've always wondered how morbidly obese people have children. I mean actually have them. How does a seven-pound baby wend its way through hundreds of pounds of fat and find the birth canal, let alone the vagina? I imagine it's like Shelley Winters in *The Poseidon Adventure*, frantically swimming for her life, looking for an escape hatch as the ship fills with water. (If you haven't seen *The Poseidon Adventure*, it's like *Titanic* without the good-looking people.) And I'm shocked that when the baby comes out it's usually healthy. I figured that the baby was so desperate to get out (to both get air and, well, it's in a vagina, yuck), it probably shot out of the snatch hatch at full force, like a hooker doing the Ping-Pong ball trick, and smashed into the wall across the room, and got all flattened and fucked up. But no, that doesn't happen;

another one of nature's unexplained miracles, like morning rain, gorgeous sunsets, and Lady Bunny's career.

Morbid obesity intrigues me on many levels. As my dear, dear, I-can't-believe-she's-not-a-drag-queen friend, Julie Andrews, once sang, "Let's start at the very beginning, a very good place to start . . ."

For über-fatties the very beginning is breakfast, which is followed by another breakfast, and another one after that. Then of course comes snack time, the three hours of noshing that will tide you over until lunches. After which comes . . . you get my point, which is: How do you get so fat that Richard Simmons drops by with a camera crew and pets you like a zoo animal? How much do you have to eat to go from being heavy to husky to what-the-fuck-happened?

As I mentioned in my reply to Janice's letter, on *My 600-lb Life*, many of the show's "stars" are so fat they can't get out of bed to get food for themselves, and rely on their spouses, children, or whoever else can fit in the trailer to bring them food. First time I saw six-year-old Jimmy dragging a little red wagon filled with two hundred Big Macs and a potato field full-o-fries into Mommy's room, I thought, "This motherfucker needs to join the teamsters. He's hauling quite a load!"

I'm also fascinated as to how fatties manage to conceive. It's a geometric phenomenon. If the wife is the bedridden mountain of meat, how does the man find the hole? Strap a GPS to his junk? (FYI, I've only seen one real vajayjay, up close, in a dirty magazine. I had no idea what I was looking at. The "model" had her legs opened to reveal a giant, hairy maw; it looked like JFK's head wound. I didn't know if I was looking at a porn picture or an autopsy photo.) And if it's the man who's morbidly obese, how does the woman get it in?

CHAPTER 2

LOVE IS A LONG AND SLENDER THING

Finally, a man I can trust.
He's so transparent.

I received A LOT of letters asking me for advice on love and romance. As I sat there, watching my assistant Jamie's fingers bleed from opening all of the envelopes, I had two immediate thoughts: 1. People have no greater understanding of the art of romance today than they did a thousand years ago, and 2. People are really stupid. They're asking ME for advice on romance and love. I'm ALONE! Three cocktails and a shirtless Zac Efron selfie and I dump a load on my Barcalounger throw pillow and pass out. What the fuck do I know about love? That said, I answered the questions with as much integrity as I could. Which, as any queen with an IQ over seventeen knows, ain't much.

Dear Bianca,

My husband says my vagina is too loose for him. What should I do?

Name withheld

Melania,

How ARE you, my love? Bet this isn't what you expected when you signed that prenup?

What should you do? Call a good lawyer in Slovenia, that's what. Might I suggest Gloria Allredczic? Until then cut a lemon wedge and put it in your pussy; sucks it right up!

Bianca,

I'm a 26-year-old pansexual girl from Australia who seems to only find gay men attractive, help me!

♥♥

Sam

Sam,

What is PANsexual? You only get moist touching a skillet? You rub Farberware all over your snatch? Even I, the Whore of Menlo Park, have no idea what you're talking about.

As for advice, not sure I can help. I, too, am attracted to gay men. Of course, as a gay man, I actually have a shot at it, while you, my Aussie jackaroo, will be left alone to tickle your fun button to old Peter Allen concert tapes. No man or gay joey will want to get into your pouch; sorry 'bout it. #FuckedUpFagHag

Dear Bianca:

I just had a baby (10 lbs., 3 oz.) and now my husband and I are dealing with post-pregnancy vagina. Your thoughts?

Robin

Milwaukee, Wisconsin

Dear Robin,

I'm not sure I'm the right person to ask, since (a) I don't have a husband; (b) I don't have a child; and (c) I don't have a vagina, but what the hell, since when has not knowing anything stopped me from opening my big mouth?

And I say "big mouth," even though my mouth is probably way smaller than your post-pregnancy vagina. I'm serious. While it's true that I can unhinge my jaw like a snake to swallow a big, meaty cock, there's no way I could push a ten-pound baby out of there.

Question one is, exactly how beat up is your mommy-pussy? Since the baby weighed over ten pounds (the size of a basketball or small sofa bed) I'm guessing the damage is fairly extensive and that your vaginal walls broke like the levees during Hurricane Katrina. Are your lips so distended that on a windy day they flap in the breeze, and you become airborne like Sally Field in *The Flying Nun*? Is your vag now so deep and wide that tourists on mules are taking tours to get to the bottom of it? If so, my advice is to call a plastic surgeon. Or FEMA. Or a green and healthy option would be to feed your vagina an organic lemon.

Question two is, WTF do you mean your husband is struggling with your post-pregnancy pussy? Struggling how? When he goes down on you does he fall in, the way Baby Jessica fell into that well? Is there an echo that's giving him tinnitus? Or is it that the walls are now so far apart his dick can't hit the sides? If that's the case, I say string a tightrope across your cooz and teach him to walk it. It'll be fun for both of you. He'll get a sense of adventure that will compensate for the lack of friction, and you'll feel like you're fucking a French acrobat instead of a produce manager from Wisconsin.

Dear Ms. Bianca,

My wife won't stop ignoring me for her tablet. All she does when she gets home is play games on it and watch YouTube videos. I try everything to make myself interesting and get her attention but to NO AVAIL! She only sees her tablet. Sometimes I feel I like I only ever see the screen in front of her face and not her. I fear I might even be forgetting what she looks like. Ms. Del Rio, I am in desperate need of your help!

Annalisa S

Dear Annalisa,

You are experiencing what is known as Lesbian Bed Death (LBD), which is when women in a committed relationship have less and less sex as the relationship goes on and on. Eventually they stop screwing altogether, gain seventy pounds apiece, bring their cats into bed, and go to sleep watching reruns of *This Old House*.

I'm sorry to say, Annalisa, but there is no cure for LBD, but it *can* be treated with vibrators, dildos, produce, or sitting on washing machines, and anything plugged into a wall (but you girls know about that already).

FYI, the term *Lesbian Bed Death* was coined in 1983 by University of Washington sociologist Pepper Schwartz. And if anybody should know about LBD, it should be someone named Pepper Schwartz. That name screams, "Not tonight; I'm too tired to lick your puss, Miriam." Or maybe it was Pepper's girlfriend, Miriam, who created the Lesbian Bed Death situation. Maybe Miriam was even more Jewish than Pepper SCHWARTZ and due to kosher dietary laws she wasn't allowed to nibble her nips while licking her lips. You know, you can't have milk with meat, and all that. How do you expect your love life to simmer when you constantly have to change pots and dishes? It's like being colored in the sixties—you don't know which water fountain to use. It's very confusing.

So, go to the store, buy a couple of good cucumbers with bumps, some baby oil, and put on Melissa Etheridge's greatest HIT. When you get home, give your girlfriend a hearty slap on the back, hope your friendship ring doesn't get caught in her hair, compliment her permed "mullet," and go into the bathroom for some special "me" time. FYI, there's always an outlet in a bathroom. Even a gay man knows that.

Have fun!
BDR

———

Dear Bianca,

I'm a brown girl. My mum wants me to find a brown guy. Where do I find them? Advice needed.

> *Mim*
> *Glasgow, Scotland*

Mim,

Wait and be patient. Between Syrian refugees, Islamic terrorists, and the Kardashians' upcoming European vacation, there'll be plenty of brown people in Scotland soon enough. Have you thought about scat? It works in a pinch.

Uncle Lou and I
are VERY close

Dear Bianca,

I just passed my driving test and my fiancé won't buy me a car! I've tried the usual "if you loved me you would…" and "OMG you don't love me!" Have I lost my spoilt bitch ways or is he just being a cunt?

Much love xx

Dear Whoever,

Yes, and yes. Yes, you've lost your bitch ways, and yes, he's being a cunt. That said, it's not too late to regain your power, girl! Have you ever read the story of Lysistrata? Oh, wait, what am I thinking? You misspelled "spoiled"; what are the odds you've read ancient Greek mythology?

Anyway, the CliffsNotes version: The women of Greece wanted the men to stop waging wars. Lysistrata, who was the most famous Real Housewife of Sparta, convinced all the townswomen to stop having sex with their husbands until they stopped fighting. In twenty minutes the gals had peace on earth and the men had a piece of puss. I suggest you do the same. Close your holes and bag your hands. Tell your fiancé, "No car, no cooz." You'll be giving him head in the backseat of a BMW faster than you can say, "Don't cum on the seats; it's a new car!"

Bianca,

How do I tell my girlfriend of four years that I'm gay?

Leo H

Dear Leo,

This is simple. Next time she's giving you a blow job, stop her and say, "No, no, no! You're not doing it right. When I suck a cock I put my left hand here and . . ." She'll be out the door before you get around to telling her what you do with your fingers.

Happy sucking!

Dear Bianca,

I can't make guys stay. We go on a couple dates and they're great, but they never stick around longer than that. Can you recommend a higher quality rope they can't chew through?

Love,
Johnny

Johnny,

You don't need a higher-quality rope; you need a higher-quality dick. If you had a better handle on how to handle your handle, maybe they'd stick around a little longer.

I once had an Asian boyfriend who was great in bed. (Okay, he wasn't really a boyfriend; he was the delivery guy from Szechuan Kitchen, but instead of me giving him a tip, he'd give me his tip. He put the soup on the table and his balls on my chin, and we'd let the [chow] fun begin!) Needless to say, he had a small egg roll, but he really knew how to use it. Beyond creative. His favorite game was Pearl Harbor. His dick was a kamikaze plane and my mouth was the USS *Arizona*. The sex was explosive! To this day, I can't watch the History Channel without popping a chubby.

Miss Bianca,

My transgender husband passed away this July. We had been together for many years before he transitioned. I was gay before he transitioned, and I am still gay now. How do I present myself as gay when I tell people my husband passed away? The assumption is that I am straight. I want to present as a gay person without having to share a seven-minute monologue about transgender and sexuality. Help!

Thanks,

Betsy

Dear Betsy,

Maybe introduce yourself as Betsy and not the Widow Betsy. Or say something like, "My husband passed away 427 days after he had his vag turned into a schlong," or "Yes, I had a husband but now I'm a purveyor of puss." Or just wear a pink pussy hat and an Ellen T-shirt.

Dear Bianca,

I just found out that my boyfriend of 2 years cheated on me with one of my friends. I brought it up to them and they both said (separately) that it was a one-time, drunken mistake. I believe them, but don't know what to do. Any suggestions?

Amy

Jacksonville, Florida

Dear Amy,

Find new friends. Find a new boyfriend. Or FUCK your boyfriend's brother AND your friend's boyfriend and call it even.

Muah xoxo

Bianca,

How do I comically come out to my Muslim parents?

Humza Ali M

To Humza It May Concern:

Do you want to make them laugh until their stomachs hurt, or until they behead you? This is a really serious question; thank ~~God~~ Allah, you've come to the right place. For who knows more about an ancient religion steeped in sexist, homophobic dogma and tradition than a tired old drag queen from bayou country?

First of all, I have no idea if you're a boy or a girl. Is Humza male, female, or a sturdy new all-terrain vehicle from General Motors? I find Muslim names very confusing. For example, here in America, we had boxing great Muhammad Ali. But we also have the comedienne Ali Wentworth. Ali was Muslim but Ali is not. See my point. (FYI, Ali Wentworth is married to ABC newsman George Stephanopoulos. And Stephanopoulos is Greek for "Ali.")

If you're a boy, don't say anything. They'll cut off your head if they find out you give head. You know those white sheets you wear out there in the desert? Start getting them in floral prints with a higher thread count. Your parents will quietly figure it out on their own.

If you're a girl, you won't have to say anything. You'll be forced to cover head to toe in heavy black burkas in the desert; you'll be sweating like a pack animal. When Mom and Dad wonder why you aren't married you won't have to open the lezzie closet. Just say, "Why don't I have a guy? Because it's eight hundred fucking degrees out here, and under this burka, I smell like a dead camel! Not even a blind cleric would want to hump."

My advice? Sit them down and say, "Mom, Dad . . . I have something to tell you. I don't want you to be mad. Don't worry, I'm not Jewish . . ." After that, anything should be okay.

———————

Dearest Bianca,

I'm sixteen years old. My older sister Donna (she's seventeen) is really pretty and I'm jealous of her. I'm decent looking, but she's way prettier. I'm tired of being called the "smart one." The "smart ones" never go out with the quarterback. They do his homework while he goes out with the pretty ones. I want to be as pretty as my sister. What can I do?

Beth
Buffalo, New York

Dear Beth,

My heart goes out to you; being the ugly sibling is never easy, just ask my sister. But I think I can help.

For starters, how 'bout a little perspective? You live in Buffalo, New York. It's a great city but not exactly a hotbed for supermodels or Playboy Bunnies. In fact, the prettiest girl in Buffalo is a divorced fifty-eight-year-old father of six, named Stosh Wasznewski. Which means either your vision of beauty has been blinded by one too many blizzards, or you're REALLY not a looker.

So, short of moving to Cleveland, where you'd be considered a ten, here are a couple of things you can do:

1. Have plastic surgery to look just like your sister.
2. Tell all the guys in your school that Donna has vaginal warts, and her cooz looks like a holiday gourd.

3. Pay your lesbian letter carrier fifty bucks to hit her in the face a coupla times with a garden shovel.

If all that fails, and she's STILL the pretty one, then change your name to Eleanor Roosevelt, marry a rich cripple, and become a lesbian yourself.

Dear Bianca,

Being gay, overweight, bald and physically disabled means I've been single my whole life and haven't had sex for over 9 years. Here's my question: How many cats can a bitter 36-year-old queen adopt before I turn into a crazy cat lady?

Miguel M
Los Angeles, California

Dear Miguel,

You say you're a bald, overweight, physically disabled, bitter old queen. That's not completely true. You're only thirty-six.

So don't give up hope. They say "there's someone for everyone." And I believe that. I'm sure that somewhere in this great country of ours there's a special man waiting just for you! It's up to you to find him. So shine your scalp, wax your belly, polish your wheels, and get going! There are fifty states to search, but I suggest you start your manhunt at the local braille institute!

Good luck, Miguel. Keep me posted. Is it okay if I give your number to Lady Bunny?

Xoxo
BDR

Dear Bianca:

My wife and I have been married for 35 years. We have two grown children who are out of the house. Since my wife went through menopause she has no interest in sex whatsoever. According to the doctors we've been to, this is not going to change. Last month I started seeing female "massage therapists," who gave me massages with "happy endings." But now I feel guilty, not happy. I don't want to hurt my wife, but I also don't want to spend the rest of my life in a loveless marriage. I don't know what to do.

Heartsick & Horny in Hartford

Dear H&H,

This is a VERY common problem among hetero, married men. Not so much gay men—but my elderly "sisters" could get a stiffie for the coroner doing their autopsies. They could get their dicks harder than their arteries.

Have you told your wife about your meetings with Happy Fingers and her fondling friends? I'm betting not. One of the things you could do is tell her. Just because her vag is bone dry doesn't mean your bone doesn't need wetting. While her legs may not be open, perhaps her mind is, and she might be okay with allowing a massage "therapist" to work the muscles in your dick. But I doubt it.

I don't believe in staying in a loveless marriage. Hell, I don't believe in staying in a loving marriage. Who wants to hit the same old hole, night after night, month after month, year after year? BORING! The first time you visit Howe Caverns it's very exciting. The second time, not so much. But the eight-thousandth time? Even El Chapo would get tired of the same old tunnel.

If your wife can't prime her pooch to prime your pump, maybe it's time to part ways. (And if you send me some hot dick pics, maybe I can be of service.)

Good luck!

B

P.S. Your massage "therapist" is about as much a "therapist" as I am an actual queen. She's just a hooker who'll rub your back before your balls. An actual queen rules over a country; I just run a drag show for old homos who have nowhere to go on Tuesday afternoons during happy hour. Don't judge.

———————

Bianca,

This past year I took part in the Women's March on Washington, and posted my pictures on Facebook and Instagram. My mother-in-law saw them and called me, demanding to know what was wrong with my marriage and "how dare I" embarrass her son. My marriage is fine, and my husband supported my marching. What should I do? I don't want to create a problem.

Nancy
Boston, Massachusetts

Dear Nancy,

Unfortunately, Princess, you already HAVE a problem; it's the old hag your hubby calls "Mommy," and it's a problem on a couple of levels.

1. Your mother-in-law, let's call her "Fuckface," assumes that because you marched with a bunch of lezzies wearing pussy

hats you're having marital problems. I'd never be caught dead in a pussy hat (I'd vote FOR domestic violence or breast cancer before I'd wear one of those things), but wearing one says you have shitty taste in hats, not husbands.

2. Fuckface thinks it's okay to call and yell at you. It's not okay any more than it's okay for you to slip the wrong meds into her soft foods at breakfast. Oops, did I say that?

3. As for "embarrassing" your husband . . . if Mr. Man isn't embarrassed by his harridan of a mother, he's surely not embarrassed by your fighting for whatever it is angry, semigroomed women fight for.

What to do? See #2. And then hide the pill bottles.

Dear Bianca:

My ex is a trans girl and I still have feelings for her, but we broke up because she wants gender confirmation surgery and I'm a gay man. Her dad has cancer right now and I want to be there for her and give her the support she needs, and I know she wants some physical comfort. How do I show her support in her current situation with her dad and her transition without sending her the wrong message? Help!!

Love you to bits.
Zach

Dear Zach,

My suggestion is, be as up-front as you can. Let your ex know that you're there for her and her father, and can offer a hand to hold and a shoulder to cry on, but not a dick to suck or a face to sit on.

Dear Bianca,

I have been married to the same man for forty years. I recently found out that he's been texting his old high school girlfriend. I'm really upset and don't know if I should leave my marriage.

Carol

Mobile, Alabama

Carol,

Leave your marriage because he's texting his ex-GF? Really? What would you do if he was fingering the old bitch, burn the house down? Kill him in his sleep? I think you're overreacting. First, if you're married for forty years, it means hubby's on the old-ish side; I'm amazed he knows how to text! My uncle Leon is seventy-three and he can't figure out how to work the fucking coffeemaker. Second, WHAT is he texting? Are the messages intimate or just social? Third, WHY is he texting her? Do YOU communicate with him and pay attention to him? And finally, don't worry about it. High school was at least FIFTY years ago. The ex-GF is an old bag; in fact, she probably shits in a colostomy bag. (Do you know how hard it is to find shoes to go with shit? You're at a fund-raiser, everything's fine, and all of a sudden, whoops, splash, your shoes don't match. How embarrassing.) My advice: ask hubby why he's texting her. His answer might be a good thing for your marriage. But if you hate his answer, then by all means, burn the house down. With him in it, of course.

Dear Bianca,

We're getting married this year. Any tips on making a gay wedding into a GAY wedding?

Andy & John
Brighton, UK

Dear Andy & John,

If you want to make it a truly GAY wedding, invite me! At your expense, of course. Fly me over first class, put me in the Ritz for five days, and provide twenty-four-hour nude room-service waiters. It'll be beyond GAY (for me and my staff of twelve). If your budget won't allow that, then go to Amazon.com, which offers an exclusive life-size Bianca Del Rio cutout available for such games as Bianca's Lashes Are Falling Down, Pin the Penis on the Drag Queen, and Poop Chutes & Ladders! If you're too cheap for that (you sent this letter standard mail and slightly damp), then, when you hit your knees, instead of praying, blow the priest. (Talk about eating the host!)

Dear Bianca,

Newlyweds here. Give us marriage advice. What's your best tip?

Adam & Laura
Wirral, UK

Dear Lovebirds,

My best tip is at the end of my dick (so I've been told, mostly by relatives—my aunt June LOVES it) and I'm guessing so is Adam's. I'm also guessing that because you're from England, Adam isn't circumcised, so you probably can't see his best tip. My advice: find a doctor or a pair of scissors or use your teeth, which, given your "heritage," I'm sure are sharp and spacious. Chomp chomp!

You're welcome.

———————————

Dear Bianca Del Rio,

My girlfriend Laurie and I are big fans of yours. Thanks for always making us laugh! Laurie and I have been together for about a year, and we're moving in together next month. There is only one thing that is a problem for me: Laurie has a huge, massive bush. It's not even a bush, it's more like a forest. It starts right below her belt line and covers her entire crotch and even goes down her thighs. I've asked her to wax, shave or even just trim it a little bit, but she refuses. She says she's beautiful the way she is. And she is, but her hairy hooch is starting to become a turnoff. Any advice? (I think if I say, "Bianca said…" she might just listen!)

Tom
Evanston, Illinois

Dear Tom,

Turnoff? It must be exhausting, chopping through the Amazon rain forest just to find the happy hole. Do you need pygmies to help you navigate the bush? Did you ever run into Dian Fossey while going down on her? Have expeditions gotten lost in her vulva?

Next time you and Snatchsquatch are getting busy, keep your iPhone next to the bed, and when you start foraging for the fun button, say, "Siri, I need directions to Laurie's vagina. I can't find it through the pubic jungle," or "Siri, I'm lost in the bush trying to find my girlfriend's twat. If I don't return, please tell my family that I love them." If that doesn't work, simply stop fucking her until she gets a grounds crew to come in and mow the lawn. Eventually she'll be so horny she'll trim her trim, and you can go in! (But send the canary in first.)

BDR

––––––––––––––––

Dear Bianca,

My husband and I are dog lovers (we have three, two Labs and a beagle) and we don't like the way our neighbors take care of their dogs. Or rather, DON'T take care of them. They leave them in their backyard all day long, even if it's raining. The dogs are left alone for 12 hours at a time, and they bark incessantly. We've spoken to them about this, and they say they love their dogs (they are well-fed and in good health) and it's none of our business. What can we do?

Janie
Kansas City, Missouri

Dear Janie,

Your neighbors are right . . . not in how they take care of their dogs, but that it's none of your business. So, what can you do? You can move. Find a house in a lesbian neighborhood; they have cats. Or move next to a bunch of Koreans; they have dogs, but only until lunchtime. Why am I bothering with your bullshit? I'm a busy woman.

Arfwiedersehen ☺

Bianca,

I have very recently started dating a cute, nice guy. Only issue is that he can't stop spilling his guts. It seems too soon in the relationship for that. Suggestions?

Alan
Ft. Myers, Florida

Dear Alan,

When you say "spilling his guts," do you mean he can't shut up about his innermost thoughts, or that he's had a discount colostomy? If it's the latter, buy slipcovers, rubber sheets, and a case of Purell. If it's the former, do what I do when dealing with someone who's had too much therapy and can't stop sharing: buy ear plugs. I have fabulous ear plugs that are invisible to the eye, but block out almost all sound. I haven't heard a word my assistant, Jamie, has said since 2004!

BDR

Dear Bianca,

I don't know if this is too personal, but here goes. I was trolling a gay bookstore recently and went into one of the booths in the back room to watch a movie. I stuck my dick through a hole in the wall and the guy in the next booth gave me a blow job. When it was over I looked through the peephole and realized the guy was my therapist. He doesn't know it was me. I have an appointment with him next week. I don't know what to do or say.

Don
New York City

P.S. One of the issues we're working on is my sexual addiction.

Dear Don,

Wow! What a sticky situation. Literally. First of all, too personal? For me??? I'll share pics of my colonoscopy with total strangers; nothing is too personal for me. I'd put my sex tapes on YouTube if only those pesky authorities weren't watching me closer than Rush Limbaugh watches the Food Channel . . . Oh, wait a minute—my publicist is frantically signaling me to shut the fuck up . . . What? Oh, I'm sorry. Did I say sex tapes? Oh, my . . . I meant fashion tapes. I don't have sex tapes. Duh. Silly me.

It's entirely possible your shrink went to the bookstore just to see a movie and the film turned him on so much he was unable to help himself (to your cock). Do you know what movie he was seeing? (*Finding Nemo*?) Okay, it's not entirely plausible. In fact, it's not even remotely plausible.

Why don't you just walk into the office and say, "Dr. Weinstein [I'm assuming], you're supposed to shrink my head, not give me head." If he laughs, you can probably keep him as your shrink. If he's ashamed and jumps out the window, you can't. No matter how this works out, look on the bright side: all those quarters are a tax write-off.

Good luck!

———————

Dear Bianca D,

I'm a Yankees fan and my boyfriend is a Mets fan. We fight constantly. Who would you root for?

Eddie
Alpine, New Jersey

MOVIES THAT SHOULDN'T BE TURN-ONS

SCHINDLER'S LIST
Yes, the yard scene in the concentration camp had lots of nudity, but still—these people were running for their lives, not the lube.

THE BAD NEWS BEARS
Children? Really? Walter Matthau? REALLY?

DRIVING MISS DAISY
It's about a ninety-year-old racist woman and her seventy-year-old black driver. Unless you're a Republican with a fetish, not exactly a panty dampener.

MY LEFT FOOT
Watching Daniel Day-Lewis slide down the steps isn't the kind of movie to jerk off to. Unless you're Jerry Lewis (no relation), in which case you'll raise money at the same time.

THE ZAPRUDER FILM
Yes, yes, yes, Jackie Kennedy crawling out of a moving vehicle in a pillbox hat (which never moved) is definitely sexy, but the plot is too dark to give most decent men a chubby.

Dear Eddie,

I'd root for Miss Louisiana. In the prelims she twirled a live gator to death to "I Kissed a Girl." Bitch is fierce. I love sports.

Bianca

Dear Bianca,

My friend's wife died a year ago, but he still uses her Facebook page (instead of creating one of his own). He doesn't post a lot, but when he does it feels creepy. I want to say something to him, but don't want to hurt his feelings. Any suggestions?

Alan

New York City

Dear Alan,

It's more than creepy, it's icky. If I want to hear from the dead, I'll talk to my ex-boyfriend's dick. Tell your friend to get off his wife's page and onto a psychiatrist's couch. And let's face it, she wasn't fun when she was alive.

Hi, Bianca,

My name is Jake and I really need advice about my partner and my family. My family mostly accepts me for who I am (gay) but they are really mean towards my partner because he has mental health issues. My family are telling me that they will never be there for me if I go ahead and marry my partner, Ben.

But I always think you should just follow your heart no matter

what anyone says. Please, Bianca, could you help me by giving me
some advice?

I LOVE YOU.
Jake

Jake,

I'm not sure if being gay is the issue or being in love with a crazy person is the issue. The gay thing is nonnegotiable. As George Hearn sang in *La Cage aux Folles*, "I Am What I Am."

Although to be grammatically correct, "You Are What You Are." Which is in love with a crazy person. I say that instead of "mental health issues," because "mental health issues" is clinical and boring, while "crazy" helps sell books.

Anyway, dating a crazy person is hard for families to accept—and rightfully so. But it's your choice, not theirs. So if you want to date a man with twenty personalities, go for it. I just hope the personality you marry is rich and terminally ill.

BDR

CRAZY PEOPLE WITH SIGNIFICANT OTHERS

CHARLES MANSON: Crazy Charlie died while I was writing this book, and I'm really pissed off about it—not because the world will miss him, but because now I have to rewrite this entry and put it in the past tense and change the timbre and tone and jokes. Less breathing for him, more work for me. Not fucking fair! Although now I can let go of the terrible resentment I've been carrying toward him. Believe it or not, at age eighty-two and behind bars, Chas had a social life. That's right—the bitch dated. In fact, a few years ago he nearly even got married. Incredible, I know. But what's truly upsetting is that Charlie was an aging maniac with a sagging swastika and crummy teeth, serving a life sentence—yet he had a love life . . . and I'M ALONE. How is that possible? I can't be *that* bad in bed . . .

THE MENÉNDEZ BROTHERS: With all due respect to Eric and Donald Trump Jr., Lyle and Erik are the world's most hideous siblings. And yet, while IN prison, they found love with women OUTSIDE of prison. Amazing. They're kind of cute and the girls don't have to worry about getting along with their in-laws.

O. J. SIMPSON: When he wasn't busy stabbing waiters or cutting off his wife's head, The Juice was dating Paula Barbieri. Whether in jail or out, The Juice's juice is still the beverage of choice for many a thrill-seeking gal.

KIM JONG-UN: Yes, the Nutbag of North Korea has a wife, Mrs. Nutbag. Not sure what the attraction is, but I'm guessing the wife is just thrilled that compared to her hubby she can never have a bad hair day.

TOM CRUISE: Yes, her again. I'm not saying Tom is mentally-ill crazy, I'm saying he's wacky in a fun way—and I'm saying that because he's known to be wildly litigious, and I don't want to get sued by the lawyers on the Scientology Spaceship. Even so, Tom has had three "wives." I'm guessing the rich and gorgeous qualities outweigh the crazy . . . I mean wacky—in a fun way!

LIZA MINNELLI: The gay icon has been married four times—and at least half of her hubbies were gay, and the others were on the spectrum.

DONALD TRUMP: Yes, yes, yes, I know, he's the president and he's rich and he has a plane and all that. But be honest—would you fuck him?

MELANIA TRUMP, MARLA MAPLES, AND IVANA TRUMP: Numbers one , two, and three.

Walking with a friend in the dark is better than walking alone in the light.

HELEN KELLER

Helen, you're in the way. Wrong person to take to a haunted house!

BIANCA DEL RIO

CHAPTER 3

PEOPLE WHO HOLD YOUR HAIR WHEN YOU VOMIT

A true friend holds your
hair when you vomit. The
downside of day drinking
is day vomiting.

Years ago, Bette Midler sang a song called "Friends." Ironic, in that that bitter cunt doesn't have any, but that's not the point. Someone else once said, "Friends are God's way of apologizing for family." I say, a friend is someone you tried to jerk off once but he couldn't get it up so you made coffee and just hung out and talked. Lots of people had questions about friendship—many of which involved the phrase *Am I obligated to post bail?* This chapter is on the ins-and-outs of friendship. And the pulling out.

Dear Bianca,

My girlfriend and I have a question for you. Let me set the scene: You promised Lady Bunny you'd help her with food shopping for a big party, but then Barbra Streisand calls you for lunch to be her new BFF, which one do you choose?

Maya & Lily
Saigon, Vietnam

Dear Ladies,

Vietnamese lesbians? You've gone from carpet bombing to rug munching; I LOVE it! This is a no-brainer. If Barbra called while I was giving CPR to a drowning toddler, Li'l Timmy better learn to swim fast. Babs waits for no one. And I mean NO ONE. And by the way, who the fuck is Lady Bunny?

Dear Bianca,

I'm a retired librarian. My husband passed away four years ago. In order to save money, I've rented out the spare bedroom in my house to a male college student. (I live near the local university.) He's a nice kid—pays the rent on time, studies, no drugs or anything like that, handsome, polite, well-mannered, etc. Problem is, he walks around practically naked almost all the time (very tight, skimpy shorts—and occasionally walks from his room to the bathroom completely naked). I'm 67 years old. I'm not sure what to do.

Lillian
Oklahoma City, Oklahoma

Dear Lillian,

Fuck him!!!

Hi! Bianca!

I'm waiting for my girlfriends to show up to day drink. So here's my question. I'm in HR and quit my job after my second kid. My kids are in day care and it's taking a while to find a job close to home. I'm looking hard, and day drinking with friends here and there. Any advice?

Lisa

Hi, Sloppy!

You don't need to be in HR, you need to be in Betty Ford. You have little kids, yet you're home day drinking … What to do, what to do … hmmmm. Well, Drunkarella, assuming you prefer rum to rehab, here's a coupla thoughts: 1. Sleep late, so the day drinking will become evening drinking and the neighbors won't be able to see you vacuuming the driveway, carrying a bottle of Stoli and a pack of smokes, or, 2. Have your favorite bartender call Social Services and remove the kids from the house. It's a win-win—the little tykes won't have to worry why Mommy's "napping" under the car, and your day drinking won't be interrupted by needy little whiners.

Hope that helps. Bottoms up! (Which I only say to alcoholics and Andy Cohen.)

Dear Bianca,

My neighbor next door always walks around his house naked, with the drapes wide open. Our houses are very close to one another with floor to ceiling windows. If he was hot it might be okay but he's not. He's old, fat and hairy. It's beyond distracting, it's disgusting. I've asked him to close the drapes or wear shorts or something, but he says it's his house, he has every right to be naked. Is there anything I can do?

> *Eddie*
> *Nashville, Tennessee*

Dear Nauseous in Nashville,

Yes, there's something you can do: pretend you're at a Ben Stiller movie and look away.

BDR

Dear Bianca:

My roommate Arlene and I moved to Los Angeles together two years ago and things were fine until recently. I have a boyfriend (she doesn't), Mark, who comes over periodically to have dinner, hang out, spend the night. Mark and Arlene get along okay. Arlene's always been introverted, but I think she's crossed the line from homebody to shut-in and it's affecting my relationships, both with her and Mark. It's been a struggle to find some private time with Mark because Arlene is ALWAYS home. Mark and I can't have a quiet dinner or cuddle up to watch a movie because she's ALWAYS there. I've asked her to give me and Mark some private time, alone in the apartment. I've asked her to go out with friends, go to a movie, whatever. I've offered to pay for her nights out, but to no avail. She just won't go out. Any advice?

Michael
Santa Monica, California

Dear Michael,

Your situation is not uncommon. Years ago, Anne Frank called me to complain that she had no privacy and that her family and roommates refused to leave the apartment. For years! Can you imagine? I don't know how Anne worked it out, I lost track of her.

Anyway, speaking with Arlene hasn't done you any good, so it's time for Plan B: kill her in her sleep. And don't forget to discreetly register with RoomateFinders.com ahead of time.

———

Dear Bianca,

My downstairs neighbors are very nice, but they talk VERY loudly, especially the father, and especially in the mornings. It's almost like they walk around with megaphones. While it doesn't usually wake me, I have to keep all the windows closed and stay in the back of the house to get away from the noise. But because I have a dog who jumps around, sometimes until 11:00 pm, and they've never, ever said a word to me about it, I feel like I shouldn't complain or say anything to them. What do you suggest?

Danny
Garden Grove, California

Dear Danny,

Unlike you, I don't have any pets . . . but I do have a lot of "foot traffic" coming in and out of my apartment late at night. And Rajib has never said a word to me about it. Not once has he passed me in the hall and said, "Hey, dick-tucker, what's up with all of the sailors and firemen?" While you and I were in similar positions, I *did* say something, because while my parade of "guests" might have made Haji nauseous, the smell of curry actually makes me vomit. I was very nice about it. I knocked on his door and said, "I know I may not be the best neighbor [big lie], but I'm actually allergic to curry [huge lie], so if you could open windows or turn on a fan when you're cooking, I'd really appreciate it." He was great; he said, "Oh, I'm so sorry. I'll take care of it." Problem solved! My suggestion to you? Lie; tell him you have a sleep disorder or a sound-related nerve condition or some other bullshit.

Hope that helps, Danny. —And oh, by the way, I offered to blow him once a week.

Dear Bianca,

I live in a gated, suburban condo complex. For the most part I have really nice neighbors. We all chat and have our dogs run and play together. Except for the guy next to me, Dan, who, for no apparent reason, just doesn't like me. Which is fine, except he's rude. Example: Yesterday, my neighbors Alan & Sue, Dave & Arlene, & Dan

We're a perfect match.
He has a six-pack, and
I just drank one!

were out playing with the dogs. When I joined we all exchanged pleasantries, except for Dan, who ignored me, as though I hadn't said hello to him. He then left. Alan asked me, "What was that about?" and Arlene said, "Who knows? He's always like that to Larry." I have zero interest in being friends with this asshole, but I don't like being publicly embarrassed for no reason. Any suggestions?

> *Larry*
> *Laguna Niguel, California*

Ahhh, Larry,

First thing you need to do is get out of the suburbs. Where I live, in West Hollywood, EVERYONE acts like Dan—snarky, cunty, and rude—but we consider those good qualities!

When dealing with jerks, my mother always used to say, "Kill 'em with kindness." Except when talking about my father, when she'd say, "Kill 'em with Clorox . . . or maybe a pillow over his head, or a not-so-gentle shove down a flight of concrete steps." I digress. Try following my mother's advice: Kill him with kindness.

Whenever you see him (especially in front of your neighbors) force him to engage with you in conversation. Be nauseatingly friendly and ask him a million questions. "Hey, Dan, how are you? Love that shirt; where'd you get it? Can you tell me the best place to buy new tires? Your garden looks great. You must have twenty different kinds of plants. Can you tell me what each one of them is, and how can I grow them?"

If he feels shame answering your questions, while he's talking, yawn really loudly for a long time, and then say, "Oh, I'm sorry. That was just sooooo boring." Then walk away.

If he doesn't answer, say to your friends, "See, I TOLD you he was an asshole." Then let your dog off the leash and sit back and enjoy while Cujo mauls Mr. Nasty Pants.

Dear Bianca,

My neighbor keeps putting Trump signs up on his front lawn and porch, and I keep taking them down. I'm getting tired. (I live in a very progressive town, and he is our neighborhood bigot.) What can I do?

Frannie
Long Island, New York

Frannie,

Acetone, carbon disulfide, lacquer, gasoline, and fuel oil are all wonderful accelerants. Wear gloves, and make sure Archie Bunker's not home at the time.

B
Xoxo

Bianca,

My best friend, Kate, and I are sharing a house. We're really close, like brother and sister. We're both in our fifties. But there's a problem: Kate says she's allergic to cleaning products so she can't do any cleaning—which would be fine, except SHE'S A SLOB! Actually, she's beyond a slob, whatever that would be. She leaves food out on the counters, dirty clothes all over the floors, doesn't clean up the dog poop in the yard, etc. I don't know if she's really allergic to cleaning products or she's just lazy, and won't do anything because she knows I'll do it. When I complain, she tells me I'm too "rigid," and should "lighten up." I don't know what to do. I just think that if she can't clean, then she can't be messy. Help!

Michael
Princeton, New Jersey

Dear Michael,

Easy. Take a giant shit in her bed. Every day. And tell her you can't clean it because you're allergic to bedding. I'm pretty sure she'll start dusting and vacuuming faster than you can say, "I had cabbage for lunch." Just a suggestion!

———————

Dear Bianca:

A talented writer friend of mine has fallen on hard times. He's facing losing his home and living out of his car. He's sixty years old, not exactly a hot commodity in the job market. Any good advice I can pass on to him?

Marla
Santa Monica, California

Dear Marla,

You're right; it is hard to get a decent-paying job at sixty years of age. Maybe he should look into being a "lab rat" for pharmaceutical companies looking to do testing for new drugs; they must pay *something,* and he'll be helping the future of mankind! And if he dies from one of the experimental drugs, well, he's a sixty-year-old homeless guy; who gives a shit?

Depending on the car, living out of it may not be such a bad idea. (Smart Car, not good; SUV, fine.) If the car has decent head and leg room—and your friend maintains a cheap membership at a gym (where he can shower, pee, poop, and cruise the steam room for casual sex with strangers—or so I've been told), his situation is quite doable. Plus, he can park on Rodeo Drive and tell people he lives in Beverly Hills! So quit being so negative; I think you're the one with the problem, Marla. FYI, on the upside, he won't be offended by this entry; he's not reading this; books cost money.

Dear Bianca:

I'm a fifty-eight-year-old gay man. My neighbor's twenty-year-old son keeps coming on to me (makes suggestive remarks, wears revealing shorts, etc.). I'm not sure what to do. The kid is really hot and I'd love for him to spend the summer in the back of my throat. I don't know if he's out to his parents or not and I don't want to ruin his family life, or make this an uncomfortable living situation for everyone. What should I do?

Michael

Danbury, Connecticut

Dear Michael,

Fuck him, suck him, let him call you Debbie and cum on your tits! Who cares what his parents think? That would be HIS problem. He's twenty, he's LEGAL, he's hot. And if he's hung, move him in.

Kisses,

BDR

P.S. I'm jealous, you old fuck.

P.P.S. SOMEONE has to diddle the children now that Michael Jackson's dead.

Dear Bianca,

My best friend, Tom, recently lost his wife after 35 years of marriage. She was almost twenty years older than he was (he was 58, she was 77) so it's not surprising she went first. It's been almost a year and I'd like to try to set him up on dates and help him get on with the rest of his life. Any suggestions on how I can be of service?

Jeff

Seattle, Washington

Dear Jeff,

If you truly want to be of service, suck his dick. You may not get a thank-you, but sometimes a good moan is more than enough.

Before I go on, I assume that when you say Tom "lost his wife," you mean she croaked, and didn't just wander off in some dementia-riddled stupor and three years from now we'll find her in a Walmart parking lot or living in the woods, like a feral cat or Nell.

You don't mention how the old lady—I'm sorry, I mean dearly departed—died. Did she die of natural causes (and by that I mean disease, organ failure, or the clichéd "fell and broke her hip, and two days later she was gone") or was it a freak accident or something a tad more sinister?

A lot of old people die in freak accidents. (I'm still amazed Blanche Hudson survived when Baby Jane pushed her wheelchair down the steps. I think her eyebrows must've broken the fall.) The old farts get their walkers stuck in a sidewalk grate and tumble into oncoming traffic; they mistake Krazy Glue for Polident; they go to give their pet dog a kiss, but forget they don't have a dog and have accidentally wandered into a wild animal preserve and gotten mauled to death trying to kiss a lion.

Or was your friend Tom so tired of trying to get it up to satisfy the withered old crone he slipped her Viagra instead of her blood pressure meds, and her heart stopped just as she was getting moist?

Unless there's an ongoing police investigation, I say it's perfectly okay for you to try to ease your friend back into the dating scene. Since he obviously likes older women, maybe throw a *Golden Girls* marathon party (although he'd likely meet more gay men than old women). Perhaps you could both start volunteering at an assisted living facility? You could be serving lunches while Tom cruises the halls looking for nana-pussy?

I think the best thing you could do is direct him toward websites and online dating sites that cater to his tastes. The ones I recommend are: guesswhoscoughing.com, #IthinkIfoundalump, and @grandmasmellsfunny. Keep me posted, and good luck to Tom!

———

Dear Bianca:

My new neighbors are from a foreign country and for the life of me I have no idea which country it is. I want to be a good neighbor and welcome them to our community but I'm at a loss; they speak a language I can't identify. Even though they're Mediterranean-looking I know they're not speaking Spanish or Italian (I have a regular gardener and a pizza guy). I don't think it's Greek or Portuguese either. My best guess is that they're Muslim and I'd like them to know that they're safe and welcome in our neighborhood. How can I find out without asking them directly, and making them either scared or uncomfortable?

Lisa
Brooklyn, New York

Dear Liberal Lisa,

Easy-peasy, my commie friend! (I AM KIDDING! You are not my friend.) Regardless of the weather, go outside in a full burka, and sit on your front porch (do you have porches in Brooklyn, or just stoops?) reading the Koran. When you see the new neighbors, if it's the woman or a daughter, wave hello; if it's the father or a son, look down at your feet (a) in shame, and (b) because you can never let a strange man look at you—you KNOW what he wants. If they respond positively, they're probably Muslim. Or you can bring them a "Welcome to the hood" basket of hummus, grape leaves, live goats, and desert sand—and wear a "Fuck the Jews" T-shirt when you swing by their place. If they smile and invite you in, then they're probably Muslim or Steve Bannon's family. Hope that helps.

———

Dear Bianca:

Our new neighbors have a large, very aggressive pit bull. We have three small children. We don't know what to do. Any suggestions?

Jim & Debbie
Los Angeles, California

Jim & Debbie,

Yes.

1. Don't send your kids to play in the yard wearing clothing made out of luncheon meat.
2. Always keep one of the children indoors, you know, as a backup.
3. If you have elderly parents or in-laws, invite them to stay with you. Even at an advanced age they're probably larger than the children, and will leave plenty of leftovers for Cujo for weeks to come.

———

Hey Bianca,

I'm 16 years of age, and at school I seem to make friends with all the seniors. When school's out for summer, all the seniors graduate and I never get to speak to them again. So please, what should I do to have friends?

Chloe
Boise, Idaho

I'm two tequilas away from buying the fat thing on the left.

Chloe,

I love that you're only sixteen and already following me! You're going to have PUH-LENTY of friends! They'll all be gay men who failed at musical theater, but they have a lot of free time to do your hair and tell you that you look pretty in your Instagram photos (which have been filtered, Photoshopped, and highlighted).

Plan A: Hang out with the dumber students; they'll never be seniors, let alone graduate. You'll be BFFs 4eva!

Plan B: Do what everyone else does: go trolling on Craigslist for friends. You might meet some great people. Of course, you might also meet a dangerous creep, which, again, might not be so bad. Think about it—which is more exciting, going to a slowly paced foreign film with some new friends, or being bound and gagged in the trunk of a Chrysler LeBaron? Try it; it's fun. Would I lie to you? A sixteen-year-old tied up in a trunk? Get real, girl, that's a Saturday night where I'm from. ☺

———

Dear Bianca,

I came home recently to find my BFF/roommate, Angie, in bed with my ex-boyfriend of five years (we broke up three months ago). Needless to say I was shocked. They say they didn't start hooking up until recently and I believe them, but I still feel betrayed. I'm a ball of conflicting emotions and I don't know what to do. Any advice?

Jennifer
Merrick, New York

Dear Jennifer,

THIS is your BFF? How low are your standards for friendship? Having a BFF like this is like having Charles Manson as your favorite family member. Anyone who would sleep with *your* ex-boyfriend in *your* house is not your BFF—or at least she shouldn't be. I'd make a laundry list of all of your friends and acquaintances and start looking to replace her. (If you want to be a bitch, start with HER ex-boyfriend.) *BFF* stands for Best Friend Forever. Angie is not your BFF, she's your BCF—and don't make me spell it out.

My advice? Either she moves out or you move out. And if it's you, (a) move out in the middle of the night, and (b) on your way out the door light a prayer candle for them . . . after you've "accidentally" doused the floor with gasoline.

———————

Dear Bianca,

Every time I have friends over, my dog immediately starts licking his balls. Help!

Nate
Taos, New Mexico

Dear Nate:

That's disgusting. Put Fido in another room. Unless, of course, when he's done licking his thing, he lights up a cigarette and sings Johnny Mathis songs, in which case you should put him on videotape and sell it to a fetish website. You may lose some friends, but it's a win-win for you and Bow-wow.

Sex is funny
and love is serious.

STEPHAN JENKINS

Sex is funny and love is serious.
And semen is hard to get out
of your hair.

BIANCA DEL RIO

CHAPTER 4

YOU'RE THE TOP!

Unicorns ARE real.
And he's hung like
a horse.

The majority of questions I received were about sex. And the majority of those questions were about fisting, toilet play, and "exactly what the fuck is it that lesbians do in bed?" And even though I've cruised every men's room, trailer park, and truck stop in America (as well as parts of Canada, Australia, and that village in Uganda where they put plates in their lips—talk about sloppy head), I am NOT an expert on sex. I'm just a cheap slut. (One year for my birthday, my Nana bought me a T-shirt that said, "Let Go of My Ears, I Know What I'm Doing." I was seven.) The sex questions covered a wide range of topics, from "How do I get my wife more interested?" to "How do I get those salad tongs out of my ass?" Enjoy!

Dear Bianca,

   I'm pregnant and any one of three men could be the father. What should I do?

Frannie
Houston, Texas

Frannie,

   Learn to give a blow job. And if you use teeth, you will NEVER be in this situation again, EVER ... Trust me.

Dear Bianca,

My husband Peter and I have been married for five years but we cannot manage to ejaculate together. What should we do?

David

Antwerp, Belgium

Dear David,

Ejaculate with other people. I'm kidding, it's obvious you're both ugly and you're not going to find anyone else.

Glad I could help.

P.S. Thanks for not submitting a photo.

Dear Bianca,

My new boyfriend and I are both 18, and we just started having sex. He shaves off all of his pubic hair and body hair, and I don't like it. He's so smooth that when we go to the beach it's like swimming with the dolphins. Even worse, he wants me to shave off my pubes and I don't want to. Any advice?

Carl

Ft. Lauderdale, Florida

Dear Carl,

I agree with you. I like pubic hair. In fact, I put it in all my meals, like parsley or cilantro! It's a real flavor saver. If you come to my house for dinner, when I say "bon appétit," what I really mean is "bone appetite!" Pubic hair is there for a reason. To catch germs, and to prevent your junk from catching fire from the friction of intense fucking. Also, it's helpful if you want to floss while sucking. (I love multitasking.)

I hate my gynecologist. He just doesn't know how to hold me.

Now, unzip
your mouth and
tell me that you
love me. Okay,
okay ... yes, it IS
Ryan Seacrest.

Since your BF's "grooming" his patch, why not bring in a stylist to do your do? Maybe a fade or a pageboy, or a clever little bob (which, by the way, is the name of a witty midget I once dated)? How about braids, so you and your BF can play German milkmaid and giant toddler?

I say compromise—he grows a little, you trim a little, and everybody's happy. And by *happy,* I mean stuck to the sheets.

Hey Bianca!

I've recently been digitizing old home videos that my dad recorded when I was a baby. One of the tapes was for my first birthday so I thought it'd be a good place to start.

After about the first hour of video, the tape suddenly jumped to what looked like a WWII American nurse standing in a bar. That nurse was a stripper. My father recorded a stripper over my first birthday. Am I good? Do I need to go jump into an ocean with concrete shoes to escape this horror?

Thanks,
Nathaniel

Dear Nathaniel,

I wasn't sure which chapter to put your letter in, the one about sex or the one about family. I decided to put it in the sex chapter because your letter is more creepy than homey.

Anyway, you're more than good. You get to watch a cute baby dribbling strained bananas down his bib, AND a busty nurse dribbling jizz down her chin. Depending on your fetishes, you could jerk off to the entire tape. And with some creative Photoshopping you could probably sell it on Amazon. I'd buy it . . . Jamie, get the credit card!

Dear Bianca,

My new boyfriend and I are totally in love—but we're also both totally bottoms. What should we do?

Alan
New York City

Alan,

I think the Yellow Pages people said it best: "Let your fingers do the walking." Seriously, how is this something that never came up in conversation BEFORE you became boyfriends? Somewhere between "Did you see Bette in *Dolly?*" and "I once saw Kevin Spacey cruising a truck stop," the words *Are you a top or a bottom?* should have tumbled out of one of your mouths. And once you figured out you were both bottoms, what made you think a monogamous relationship would work? How stupid are you?

FYI, *monogamous* is the key word in that last paragraph. Because in my opinion, unless you boys are happy with dildos, vibrators, cucumbers (fresh, farm-to-market), baseball bats, flagpoles, or NutriBullet, this is never going to work out.

I suggest you find a mutually agreed-upon third party with a big, serviceable dick, and let him pound your pussies while you two moan, cry, bite the pillows, and call out each other's name. I hear Michael Fassbender, Liam Neeson, and Whoopi Goldberg are available (in no particular order).

Dear Bianca,

A couple of newlyweds moved into the apartment next door to me. I can hear them when they're having sex (which is all the time), especially her. She's a screamer. Bloodcurdling shrieks for hours on end. What should I do?

Jeff
New York City

Dear Jeff,

First, be grateful and quit being a cunt. You can afford to live in New York. Alone! Maybe she's screaming 'cause she opened the rent bill. You want a real problem, how about when you smell food for days in the hallway only to find out no one was cooking. Your neighbor was dead. Once you experience that, we'll finish this conversation.

Fondly,

BDR

Bianca,

My boyfriend came out as a trans woman, but I'm still a straight cis woman. Any catchy term for a straight girl dating a trans woman?

Jenny
Dallas, Texas

Jenny,

What a thoughtful question! I have such compassion for you and your situation. I hope you can soldier on and work this out. But to answer your question, the catchy term for a straight girl dating a trans woman is *loser*.

Dear Bianca,

My boyfriend has a pencil dick. What should I do?

Dave

Austin, Texas

Dear Dave,

Practice your penmanship. And have a cigarette! Your letter shocked me; I thought everything was bigger in Texas. ☺ Seriously, if your boyfriend's tiny tool is causing trouble in your relationship then I think you need to sit down and have an honest talk with him. Over a glass of Chardonnay, you could say, "Ling Cho, I love you very much, but our sex life is no good. When I'm ass-up, your gherkin ain't hurtin'! Maybe we could bring in a third party to spice things up? Someone with a bigger dick than yours; you know, some guy who's packin' four or five inches." Honesty is the best policy, Dave. I hope that helps.

If not, once a week tell him you're going bowling and instead go loiter in a filling station men's room in a black neighborhood.

Xoxo

BDR

Dear Bianca,

Would you rather fuck your grandmother or lose your penis?

Ed

Chicago

No discussion. Yes.

(Thankfully, weight gain has no effect on dick size. If Michael Fassbender gains three hundred pounds, his knob will still be dragging along the floor like a Swiffer.) I assume the woman gets on top, otherwise we're looking at a bone-breaking, junk-yard-car-crushing scenario. I've often wondered (and by that I mean obsessed over) if Ellen Barkin's flattened features were a result of letting her fatass ex-husband, Ron Perlman, use her face as a lawn chair. Whatever; Ellen is still hot, so maybe chubby-chasing has its upsides; who am I to judge?

I could go on, but all this fat-shaming is making me hungry.

Love means never having
to say you're sorry.

ERICH SEGAL

Love means never having
to say, "That's just a cold
sore, right?"

BIANCA DEL RIO

Dear Bianca,

I have a hypothetical question: Would you rather watch your parents have sex every day, or join in once, just to stop it?

Jeri

Newark, New Jersey

Dear Jeri,

Hypothetical, schmypothetical. Someone got a little too close to Mommy and Daddy during their special grown-up time, didn't they? That's a tough question. For starters, what do Mommy and Daddy look like? If they're fat and disgusting, like most parents are, go in the bathroom RIGHT NOW and throw acid in your eyes. You're much better off learning braille and crossing the street with a guide dog than ever seeing that again.

If they're hot, I'd say watch every day and "accidentally" film it with your phone. Then you can "accidentally" sell it online. If they're fat and hideous, you can "accidentally" film it with your phone and "accidentally" sell it to TLC for one of their freak series. And if they're brother and sister, you can "accidentally" film it with your phone, then go to Arkansas and "accidentally" sell it to the Christian Broadcasting Network. And if they're REALLY hot, join in. But why only once? That's no fun. From what I hear, Jeri, Mommy's a cumdumpster. And Daddy's a party bottom!

Bianca

P.S. Is that Jeri as in "Hall" or "Curl"? Honestly, I kill me!

Hey Bianca,

I'm 21 and a virgin and I am extremely scared of losing my virginity!! How do I stop myself from being so cock shy? Genuine question. I am TERRIFIED!!

Cheers love ☺

Florence M

Dear Florence,

Up until now, the most disturbing letter I received was from a young mother whose twin boys were eaten by lions when they fell into the Big Cats cage at the local zoo. But your letter is waaaaay more upsetting. Twenty-one and STILL never been laid? How is that possible? Mother Teresa was sucking dick by fifteen. And the lad was a leper. "Melts in your mouth, not your hands."

Are you afraid because you think it will be painful the first time? If so, there are plenty of ways to break your hymen BEFORE you ride a cock. How about riding a horse? How about riding a bike with no seat? How about taking a yoga class and assuming the position "Downward Facing Loser"?

Having sex the first time is like swimming—you just have to dive in and hope for the best. What's the worst that will happen? It'll hurt? You'll get pregnant? You'll get syphilis and go blind? So what? Nothing worthwhile in life is without risk.

Go with the flow, Flo, go with the flow!

P.S. Don't do it when you have a flow!

Dear Bianca,

My friends and I like to play a party game called "Describe Your Sex Life in a Movie Title." I realize this isn't really asking for advice, but… If you could sum up your sex life in a movie title, what movie would it be?

Danny
West Hollywood, California

Dear Danny,
    JAWS. Nuff said.

Dear Bianca,

My boyfriend likes butt stuff, so I wanted to get him a butt plug or something. But they're too expensive, so I found a dog toy at the dollar store that resembled one.

He loves it and always wonders where I bought it because he wants to buy another like it. Should I tell him it's a dog toy?

Carol
Norfolk, Virginia

Dear Carol,

If his ass squeaks when he farts, he already knows it's a dog toy. I say absolutely buy him another one. And another one. And another one after that. If he likes all this doggie stuff, sooner or later you won't have to blow him, because he'll have learned to lick himself. You can scratch his ears, shove a toy up his butt, and go out shopping with your girlfriends. When you come home, the deed will be done and all you'll have to do is say "Good boy," and give him a cookie!

You know, I have a date tonight but I don't feel like waxing or shaving. Think I'll stop at Petco on my way to the restaurant. Thx for your letter! ☺

I have a question for *you*. Is a flea collar S&M, a medical necessity, or just an accessory?

———

Hey Bianca!

My boyfriend is trying to fist me, but we keep getting stuck at the last knuckle on his thumb. He's 5'5" and female-to-male trans, so his hands are pretty damn small already. Any advice on how to get it in?

Love,
Jared

Dear Jared,

Only 5'5"? I thought Ivanka was way taller than that. Besides which, don't tiny hands run in the family?

The problem isn't your boyfriend's hands; the onus is on your anus. Time for a stretching exercise—kind of like a reverse Kegel.

Your asshole sounds like the WiFi in a train station—a long, dark tunnel with service that goes in and out. Since his "penis" hasn't loosened you up, I suggest you try various fruits and vegetables; it's the healthiest option. Start with frozen peas, tiny carrots, and baby cucumbers and work your way up to celery stalks and giant eggplants. Have a healthy hole! (FYI, don't try this AT the supermarket. It's been my experience that produce managers are judgmental bitches.)

If that doesn't work, go to your local shoe repair shop and offer to blow the cobbler if he'll let you borrow his shoe widener. Have a couple of cocktails and let your ass take a walk on the wild side.

You're SO welcome!

———————

Hi Bianca,

I'm James, I'm 23, and my partner's 22 and pregnant with my baby. We got together while she was pregnant with an ex's baby after he told her it was either their relationship or the baby (a beautiful boy). But me and my partner suffered a miscarriage last year and now we've found out she's pregnant again, and as happy as I am, I am also terrified that she may miscarry again. I'm worried that there is something wrong with me (my mum can't carry girls). I'm worried that I have defective sperm or something. I'm a big fan and I'm normally a lot like you—tough but kind to those I like (I'm an absolute cunt to those I hate)—so I just really want some advice from someone with your experience and look forward to hearing from you.

James
Newcastle upon Tyne, UK

James,

While I appreciate your compliments, you're nothing like me; I'm an absolute cunt to people I actually like. Now back to your problem. "Defective sperm" won't cause a miscarriage. Once the sperm fertilizes the egg, its job is over—just like Adore Delano, whom I beat to win *Drag Race*. Last I heard, the poor thing was spritzing perfume at a

Macy's in Oxnard. James, there are a lot of reasons for a miscarriage, but don't blame yourself; blame your girlfriend. It's HER uterus, for fuck's sake.

What intrigues me about your letter is that you hooked up with your partner while she was pregnant (with someone else's baby). I don't care that it was someone else's baby, I care that she was pregnant. That is some kind of crazy. It's also some kind of fetish, preggophilia to be exact. That's when a man (or woman) is attracted to a pregnant woman. Now, you don't say how pregnant she was when you hooked up—first trimester? Second? Third? Was the baby crowning? If it was a later term, then you could have been sticking your dick in your GF's vagina AND in the baby's mouth. Technically, you'd be getting laid AND blown at the same time! Some people might think of that as creepy and weird—not me. I think of it as a three-way and at a really inexpensive family discount!

I hope your partner has an easy pregnancy and gives birth to a beautiful, healthy baby. And if not, I hope the baby is freakish enough that you can make money off it.

Dear Bianca:

I've gone on two dates with a guy that I really like. We haven't gotten intimate yet, but we've talked about our turn-ons and things like that, so I know it's coming. He told me he has a foot fetish and really, really, REALLY likes beautiful, sexy feet. I lost three toes in a lawn mower accident a few years ago, and don't know how to tell him. Should I give him a heads-up, or just wait for the moment we get physical and hope he doesn't mind?

Dan
Altoona, Pennsylvania

Dear Dan,

The first thing that comes to my mind is, UCCCH! Second thing is, never, ever, ever wear open-toed shoes. You might consider asking him to define *beautiful, sexy feet*. Find out exactly what that means to him. If he says "a full complement of toes," then you need to tell him that three of your little piggies went off to the market. But if his foot fetish sounds more fetishy than you originally thought, then keep your mouth shut—and hope that he likes surprises!

Xoxo

BIANCA'S FAVORITE FETISHES

Everyone knows about the average garden-variety sexual fetishes, like voyeurism and bondage and baby talk and leather (although I've never quite understood the leather thing. Do you only get turned on by leather clothes—vests, chaps, hats—or do you pop a chubby in discount furniture stores or in the waiting rooms of Mexican doctors' offices?), but there are puh-lenty of other, lesser-known fetishes that intrigue me:

AVISODOMY: Has nothing to do with rental cars, but everything to do with chickens, hens, turkeys, and capons. Avisodomy is sexual intercourse with poultry, or as I like to think of it, the Pluck-n-Fuck, or Chick-fil-Laid. I don't know if the birds are alive or dead when they're getting stuffed, but I do know why Colonel Sanders keeps licking his fingers.

GERONTOPHILIA: Sex with old people. Nana-banging. When it's over, does your partner remember whose name to call out? Does he yell, "Was it good for me?" Look at the bright side: If a man has a foot fetish and a nana fetish, imagine how much fun he must have when she takes her bra off and her tits hit her toes.

MUCOPHILIA: Exactly what it sounds like—an attraction to mucus. So attention, emphysema sufferers—chins up! Somewhere there is a special someone waiting for you to hock a loogie all over them!

PSELLISMOPHILIA: Arousal to stuttering. "I'm gonna c-c-c-c-c-c-c-c-cum."

COPROPHILIA: An arousal to feces. I don't get this at all. For starters, I NEVER wear earth tones. Second, what kind of shoes do you wear with loose stool? I'm guessing that if you tell a coprophiliac to "go shit in your hat," not only will they do it, but then they'll put the hat on, at a jaunty angle, like Sinatra, or parade around like Audrey Hepburn in *My Fair Lady*. They'll stink, but they'll strut.

COULROPHILIA: Sexual attraction to clowns. (And I don't mean Donald Trump, I mean real, honest-to-God clowns, like Bozo or Ronald McDonald.) I kind of get it (look what / look like). You know what they say about a man with big shoes . . . Ronald McDonald is, of course, the spokes-clown for Ronald McDonald House, which helps children with cancer. Can you imagine being turned on by both circus clowns AND sick kids? Wow! That's more than a weird fetish, that's a fabulous weekend. Or maybe a long-term stay at Bellevue or Rikers Island.

Family is the most important
thing in the world.

PRINCESS DIANA

Seat belts, a clear tunnel, and
a driver who's not drunk are
more important than family.

BIANCA DEL RIO

(WE MISS HIM . . . OH, AND HER TOO)

CHAPTER 5

FUCK FOSTER CARE!

You've probably noticed that all of the previous chapters (as well as the following ones) have photos at the beginning, but this chapter—on family—doesn't. Assuming you're not passed out on the floor and covered in either cheap liquor or jizz, you're probably wondering why. I can answer that for you, but why should I? Isn't it enough that I wrote this whole fucking book? I'll let you figure out why there are no photos of me in this chapter. Here are your choices:

* No person on earth wants to claim me as family.

* I was hatched.

* All of my family members are currently serving time.

* I'm a NASA experiment gone wrong.

* I was raised by wolves.

* The cave drawings didn't survive the Stone Age.

* Court records are sealed.

* I don't want my family finding me and begging for royalties.

* The Manson family might claim me as their own.

* Ever see *Deliverance*?

* It has nothing ... I repeat, NOTHING ... to do with that incident in the church bathroom with my cousin.

* Photos are expensive. I had to draw the line somewhere.

* The only family photos I have are dick pics.

Family Feud. Family Affair. Family Time. Family Values. Family Van. Family Room. Family Hour. Family, family, family . . . Fuck families! I am sick of them! Yet, many of you are not. In fact, you sent me thousands of letters seeking family advice. So I put on my big-girl pants, knocked back a couple of 40s, and answered all the family questions that didn't completely bore the shit out of me.

Dear Bianca:

My new neighbors, let's call them Kevin and Maureen, have a teenage son—let's call him John—who is obviously gay; obvious to everyone but them. John is beyond flamboyant; he's nellier than all of Liza Minnelli's husbands put together (may three-quarters of them rest in peace). Yet Kevin and Maureen are clueless. They keep pushing John to get involved in sports and hiking and other outdoorsy shit, and try to set him up on dates with girls. They have no idea that John doesn't want to have a girlfriend, he wants to be a girlfriend. Needless to say, John's quite upset by all of this; he's taken out his rage on his Barbie collection, and ripped all the hair out of the dolls. He has 22 bald Barbies. He tried to pass it off with a joke, saying, "It's Chemo Barbie, and she's given up her Dream House for a semi-private room at Sloan-Kettering!" I want to help the boy but don't know what to do. What do you think?

Bridget
Orange County, California

Bridget:

First of all, the son—let's call him John . . . Travolta (also bald)—is in a situation many gay teens deal with. He has (I hope) well-intentioned but oblivious parents, coupled with an incredible desire to suck black dick. (I'm projecting here, but what are the odds I'm completely wrong? Name one gay boy who hasn't thought about going to Browntown for a slurp session? I have; it was prison related, but I digress.)

Before I go on, it's important to note that John's coming-out process is none of your business. That said, let's butt the fuck in, shall we? As a self-righteous faggot who knows a thing or two about wigs (speaking of cancer, and hair choices), it's my MORAL OBLIGATION to help.

Does John know *you* know he's a homo? If so, great. If not, you should let him know you know he likes playing the skin flute. Maybe next time you see him on the street, you can compliment him by saying something like, "John, I love your dimples! Or are those ball marks?" Or invite him to dinner and say, "We're having sausage tonight. They may not taste great but they'll look good going into your mouth." Once he knows you know, you can be his safe harbor: you can offer him an ear to listen, a shoulder to cry on, a muumuu to slip into. (Google "Mrs. Roper.")

As for the parents, let's call them Tweedledum and Tweedledenial—that's a whole 'nother story. If Johnny's as faggy as you say he is (and I say that in a good, loving, "Wow, you came fast; can you go again?" kind of way), chances are they already know. (Surely, the Barbie collection tipped them off.) The parents ALWAYS know. I remember when I "came out." Mom and Pop came downstairs to my room, kicked open the door, and my mother said, "Your father and I know you're gay!" I was so stunned I didn't know what to do. So I got up from the sling chair, took off the nipple clamps, unzipped my mouth, and said, "Do you still love me?" My father started gently weeping and said, "Of course we do, faggot! Just don't spill your lube on the carpet." I daresay, I was the happiest nine-year-old on the block. (This story is totally untrue; I've never met my father.)

Sometimes, parents don't want to know. A lot of times they think their son/daughter is just "experimenting." I believe that the rule is if you do it once, you're drunk; twice, you're curious; three times, you're a Republican congressman with a wife and four happy Christian children.

I also hear that a lot of parents think their child's gay behavior is a "phase." News flash: a phase doesn't last four decades. Unless you're Cher.

Families sometimes use euphemisms to help them with their discomfort. When I was five years old, I asked my grandmother why my uncle Robert wore a mink coat and carried a pocketbook. She said, "Because he's musical." I said, "Nana—Uncle Robert is sixty-three, wealthy, lives with six cats and a Cuban pool boy, and he doesn't have a pool. I don't think he carries a pocketbook because of music." She said, "No, he carries it because you never leave your purse around a Cuban. Whatever, faggot. I love you."

Bridget, if you want to help John, why not chat up Kevin and Maureen, and tell them how quirky and funny and wonderful their son is? And then, since I'm assuming they're Catholic (Kevin and Maureen? Jews? I think not), maybe welcome them to the neighborhood by bringing them to the local church for a Sunday mass. They can make new friends and reconnect with God, and John can have a gang bang with Father Joe and his slow-witted boyfriend, I mean altar boy, Dennis. Sounds like a win-win to me! By the end of the day, Johnny will be flaming more than the "purse."

Dear Bianca,

After I moved to a small apartment a few years ago, I agreed to loan my sister an antique cabinet that wouldn't fit in the apartment. Well, fast-forward to now—I bought a house and asked for the cabinet back. When my sister returned it, it was beat to shit and one of the legs was broken. I'm not sure if I'm more upset that it came back damaged, or that my sister hasn't said anything, let alone offered to pay for the repair.

Andrea B
Rhinebeck, New York

Dear Andrea,

First off, isn't Rhinebeck a granola-backpack-Birkenstock kind of town? I haven't been there in years, but if I remember correctly, it's a quaint little grotto on the Hudson River, chock-full of pottery shops and lesbians. If you want your cabinet repaired I'm sure there are plenty of handy gals about town who can fix it up in a jiffy! But why bother? I say, save your money and make up a fabulous story about how it got damaged. Maybe something along the lines of, "I lent it to Pamela Anderson and she got drunk and mistook one of the legs for Tommy Lee's dick..."

FYI, I can't tell you the number of times I've been returned to the shelter beat to shit with a broken leg. Please, bitch, at this point my legs have been broken so many times I can barely summon the emotional strength to laugh at telethons.

Dear Bianca,

    I have two children (ages 9 and 10); my brother also has two children. We live on opposite sides of the country and at Christmas time we always meet at our parents' home, which is about halfway between, to celebrate the holidays. For some odd reason my parents are nice to my brother's children, but not very nice to mine. My kids have noticed and don't want to go to Grandma's house this Christmas. What do you think?

                    Marilyn
                    Flint, Michigan

Marilyn,

    Christmas is the least of your worries. You live in Flint; your children are drinking poisoned water. I'm pretty sure this problem will resolve itself in no time. Besides, you can have other kids. Maybe your parents will like them better than your current litter.

Dear Bianca:

    Ok this is going to be a question asked by so many people.

    How do I come out to my dad as being gay when he is very homophobic? Let me just quote, "I'd like to kill all the homos."

    Thank you and I hope for your reply.

                    Love you x
                    Joey A

Dear Joey A,

You are soooo right. I was asked this question by soooo many people. Totally unoriginal and tedious on your part. But, since I have to answer at least one of them, why not yours, right? (Your name sounds very southern, and the fact that your dad seems to be a gun aficionado makes you the one whose generic letter I've decided to answer.)

First of all, your letter is kinda vague. You don't say how old you are. If you're forty-eight and still afraid to have this talk with your daddy, then coming out is the least of your issues.

Secondly, your father isn't homophobic; he's an asshole. A phobia is an unnatural fear of something. Your father isn't afraid of homos, he doesn't like them. Not the same thing. HomoPHOBIA would be if he was afraid that a gay burglar would break into the house and rearrange the throw pillows. Your father actually wants to shoot homos. A person who has a fear of heights, acrophobia, is afraid of flying in planes. He doesn't necessarily want to kill all pilots and flight attendants.

I don't think a casual "Hey, Dad, I need to talk to you" chat is going to do you any good. I suggest you come home with a huge, hairy biker bear, who has tattoos, body piercings, and an ugly scar running down his entire face. You walk in the door and say, "Hi, Dad, this is my new girlfriend, Buck." Pops will either be too afraid to spew his hatred, or so stunned he'll have a heart attack and drop dead. Think of it as a win-win.

Note: I don't want you to think my reply is original; I must confess it was on an episode of *Forensic Files*, which I consider the feel-good show of 2017.

Dear Bianca,

My sister recently had lap band surgery and has lost almost 200 lbs. She's looking much better (she originally weighed 360) and seems a lot happier. I'm thrilled because I love her a lot. My issue is that when she's asked about the weight loss she says she did it with diet and exercise, which is a lie. And when she says it to people in front of me, or people we both know, it makes me complicit in the lie. That makes me very uncomfortable. Any advice?

Eleanor
San Antonio, Texas

Dear Eleanor,

You act like you've never lied. Cut it the fuck out. EVERYONE lies. When our first president, George Washington, said, "I cannot tell a lie," he was lying. The Big G lied plenty. For example, he didn't actually chop down the cherry tree, he had his gardener, José, do it. He confessed because he didn't want Martha to know he was banging José's sister, Juanita. (Who, by the way, had a baby with George. How Martha never noticed that her son Paco's first words were *mamacita* and *inmigració* is beyond me.) Our current president, Donald Trump, lies every 3.7 seconds. It doesn't bother him in the least, and it doesn't bother his family either. (*His* sister isn't writing to me complaining about the lying, is she?) So let go of the integrity bullshit; if your sister wants people to think she lived on salads and treadmills, let her. Besides, six months from now, when the lap band breaks and she burps up a turd, they'll know the truth anyway.

Dear Ms. Bianca,

I'm a thirty-four-year-old single gay man. My first cousin, Sharon, lives in Texas. She's great and I love her and her kids. But her husband, Charlie, is homophobic. He won't let me see the children because he thinks all homosexuals are child molesters, which is, of course, ridiculous. I've spoken to Sharon and she's in a tough spot. She knows her husband's being an idiot, but he's the father of her children and they're happily married.

I don't know what to do. Any advice?

Andrew
Florida

Dear Andrew,

Wow. This situation is harder than Chris Christie's arteries. For starters, understand that they live in Texas, a state that elected Rick *Dancing with the Stars* Perry governor, twice. Not exactly a state-full-o-thinkers.

Everyone knows that, proportionally, heterosexuals are WAAAAAAY more likely to be child molesters than gays. Everyone except Charlie, that is. I fear nothing that you, Sharon, friends, family, scientists, doctors, or experts say is going to change his delusional mind. But a lawyer might! I say, sue the motherfucker for every penny he has, for defamation of character, character assassination, and anything else the lawyer can think of. The goal is not to win money but the opportunity to see your nieces and nephews. Let Sharon know what you're doing and why you're doing it.

You're not allowed to see the kids now, so what have you got to lose? And who knows, if you win, maybe Charlie will see how fabulous you are and change his mind! (I'm assuming you're fabulous; don't prove me wrong by showing up in court wearing pleats, or a cotton-poly blend.)

———

Dear Bianca,

My brother got married last year, for the second time. (His wife, and mother of his two kids, ran off a few years ago.) His new wife is a sloppy alcoholic (slurred language, bad driving, spilling things, falling down) but both she and my brother are in denial about it. Everyone else in the family—and neighborhood—is aware of it. My problem is that his kids (ages 8 and 10) are starting to ask me questions about her behavior. What should I tell them?

Andrea

Levittown, Pennsylvania

Dear Andrea,

This sounds verrrry familiar. Jamie, is this you? Wait a minute, am I being punk'd? Never mind, back to your question.

Sounds like an episode of *Will & Grace*, except without the jokes and the homos. Right up front, let me say that I'm pretty sure your brother knows he married an alkie; a "normal drinker" doesn't consider vomit an accessory.

You should tell the children the truth, that their new mommy's real name is Jackie Daniels, she's a cheap drunk, and after a couple of shots and a six-pack, she'll hop up on the pool table and give everyone in the bar a turn. But use nicer language (they are children, after all). For example, change "cheap" to "broken down," and "six-pack" to "a keg of brewskis."

Your brother may get mad at you, but in the long run you'll be doing him a favor. And the kids will learn (a) about problem drinking, and (b) how to mix a martini without bruising the gin!

———————

Dear Bianca,

My stepdaughter is eleven, going on twelve, and she still sleeps in bed with me and her father. This began long before I came on the scene, and while I understand that she's close to her dad, she's getting to the age where it's becoming uncomfortable. Any advice?

Bonnie
Des Plaines, Illinois

Dear Bonnie,

Move to West Virginia, where it's legal to do that shit.

Xoxo

P.S. I hate the expression *eleven, going on twelve*. Of course she is, twelve follows eleven. She can't be eleven going on thirty-eight, can she? If she's not "eleven going on twelve," then her only option is to be "eleven going on dead," and we'd hate that, wouldn't we? But it would get the needy skank out of the bed. Win–win. ☺

———————

Bianca,

We were looking through our seventeen-year-old son's phone the other day, and we came across this app called Grindr. Apparently, it's a dating site for gay men. We were shocked! Does this mean he's gay? Could he be going through a phase? Is this something all the kids today do? We want to say something to Robert, but don't know what, or how to approach the subject. Any suggestions?

Mary & Joe
Cincinnati, Ohio

Dear M&J,

Yes! Mind your own fucking business!!! Why were you looking through his phone? He's seventeen, for fuck's sake, not seven. How about a little privacy? In the modern world (and by *modern* I mean post-1985; catch up, you snoopy pricks) phones are like diaries: people keep their most private thoughts on them. Would you read Robert's diary if he had one? (If he's gay, he might have one. Gay boys love to journal, when they're not dancing, cruising, or snorting meth in their BFF's garage. You know, if Anne Frank were alive today her diary would be an app, and she'd be swimming in money; certainly enough to pay off the Nazis.)

Yes, Grindr is a dating app for gay men. Does this mean Robert is gay? How would I know, he's never sucked my dick. If you want to know if he's gay, but don't want him to know that you're nosy pigs, with no boundaries or respect for privacy, wait until the next time he says he's going "hunting for bears." Pay attention to see if he's carrying a rifle or a black handkerchief and a bottle of K-Y. Then learn to MYOB!

Dear Bianca,

A lot of gay men have parents who aren't very understanding or tolerant. I have the opposite problem. My parents are TOO gay friendly. In fact, they're so gay friendly they're driving potential boyfriends away. HELP!

Smothered in San Diego

Dear Smothered,

How awful. Overly loving parents; you have to pretend to be nice to THREE people, instead of just one, uggh! (When I'm on a date with a guy, I always act nice—almost like I'm someone else, so he'll get to know the real me.) It would be much simpler if you had hateful, homophobic, Christian parents so you wouldn't have to deal with them at all. But you don't. You're stuck with Nick and Nora Nice, who want you to be happy. What's that all about?

Anyway, I'm assuming you've talked to them about the suffocating lovefest and it hasn't done any good. My advice? Have a fun movie night at home! You and your current BF, Little Timmy (why not?), should make a nice dinner, and then you and LT and your parents snuggle up on the couch and watch movies. Gay porn movies. Hard-core gay porn movies. Starring you and Not So Little Timmy. I'm pretty sure Mom and Pop will leave you alone after that. Because while they want to see you happy, they don't want to see you getting fisted. But I do. My PO box is . . .

Hope that helps!

Xoxo

Moi

P.S. You know what I hate? When faux-Christians say, "Hate the sin, love the sinner." That is such bullshit. That's like saying, "I hate shrill, awkward, lip-syncing Canadians, but I love Céline Dion." No, you don't. You can't stand her. You can't hate felching and then be all kissy-face with the felcher. Just sayin'. Glad I got that off my ~~chin~~ chest.

———

Dear Bianca,

I'm Claudia and write from Rome, Italy. My question is: how to explain to my 2 and ½ years old daughter what's the meaning of gay? I wasn't embarrassed nor scared, but trying to be clear I had to use words like "normal" and "usual" for the heterosexual love. The fact is that the baby understood quite well the meaning (I ended with an "isn't important if you love a male or a female, love is always a beautiful thing" and she said "oooook") but I'm asking to myself if I somehow transmitted—with the words, not with the intentions— that the gay love is not normal, is not usual. Maybe it's only my paranoid... but I really want to teach her how love and respect is fundamental, no matters about gender or color or thoughts.

Hoping not beeing so heavy for you to read... and sorry for my bad english!

I would reeeeeeeeally like to see you in Rome, meanwhile I'm trying to emprove my english watching RuPaul's drag race seasons on and on.

With love and respect,
Claudia

Dear Claudia,

Ciao! (Which I've learned means both "hello" and "good-bye" in Italian, the way "Shalom" means "hello" and "good-bye" in Hebrew, and "Get the fuck out!" means "hello" and "good-bye" in Boston. What can I say, I'm trilingual! Yet another reason to love me. I'm like the fag whisperer.)

In this book, I've edited many of the letters for a variety of reasons—time, space, fluidity, etc. (as well as for grammar and spelling, so that my many fans don't look like ignorant dopes), but I left your letter exactly as it was written. Not because it's charming or special, but because my readers will appreciate my patience in wading through pages of typos, poor usage, and dangling participles.

Claudia, why are you explaining gay love to a two-and-a-half-year-old? Aren't potty training and teaching her not to put foreign objects (bottle caps, sticks, Aunt Luisa's vibrator) in her mouth higher priorities at this age? I realize that Europeans are way more advanced than Americans (on *Sesame Street,* Oscar the Grouch isn't explaining to the kids why he's never been married, or why he shares his garbage can with a slender, blond boy named Trevor) but this is a little much. When your daughter starts asking about sex or love, or will only eat fish for dinner, that is the time to have this conversation. Until then, don't worry about what message you sent—she was too busy wondering about her coloring books to pay attention to you. Leave her alone—shave your legs, wax your lips, and learn to make ice.

———

Dear Bianca:

My sister's husband is cheating on her . . . with a male UPS driver. I'm gay and was in the closet for years, so I understand my brother-in-law's situation and empathize with him. But I love my sister and think she should know what's going on—before they have children. Any advice on what to do?

Dan
Seattle, Washington

Dear Dan,

This situation is stickier than Lady Bunny's panties on a summer day in Miami. Take a moment to envision that and try not to vomit.

A couple of things to consider before you say anything: 1. Your sister may already know her husband's a sister; 2. Your sister might be half a dyke herself (is her favorite color plaid?); 3. They may have an open relationship and they're each allowed to do their own thing, or do their own delivery person. None of this, of course, is any of your damn business. Although if the answer is number 3, I'd ask hubby if you can borrow the UPS guy. Why not find out what brown can do for you? Hopefully he won't mishandle your package.

Healing, no?

———————

Dear Bianca,

I hate my wife's nine-year-old son. He's rude, obnoxious and mean. We have joint custody and the boy spends 50% of the time with his father. What can I do so that he stays with his father 80% of the time?

> *Bob*
> *Raleigh, North Carolina*

Dear Bob,

Molest him. You'll get to 100 percent in no time.

———————

Dear Bianca:

I've been bitterly estranged from my family for a number of years, including my mother and my three siblings (and their families).

My mum recently died and I don't want to go to the funeral. I also
don't want to feel guilty about not going. I had a terrible relationship
with my mum (I was a battered child) and want nothing to do with
my brothers and sister. Any advice?

David

Ealing, London, UK

Dear Dave,

I'm sorry about your mother's death . . . unless, of course, she was
a *total* cunt, in which case I'm happy for you. By the way, on a scale of
one-to-Katherine Heigl, exactly how cunty was she?

Funerals are for the survivors; the dead person is dead. (Unless
the dead person is Shirley MacLaine, who keeps coming back, like
jock itch, acid reflux, or those horrible Fast & Furious movies.) So,
if you're considering going to the service for your mother's sake,
remember, she's DEAD; someone dropped a house on her. If you
don't want to see your siblings, then why go? How good could the
catering be?

It seems to me there are only two reasons to even consider going:

1. You're in the will and will collect a lot of money (if the old bag
   had any, and I say that in a kind, loving way).
2. You want to upset your siblings by creating a scene (i.e.,
   showing up at the church naked, vomiting into the open
   casket, giving the priest a hummer in the confessional, etc.).

If either of those is true, then pull that black suit out of the closet,
and go enjoy the festivities! Don't be a stick-in-the-mud, like she's
soon to be. (And remember, she's your only mother, you don't get the
chance to bury the bitch twice.)

Hey Bianca =),

I need your sass and advice on something please.

I'm not gonna take the scenic route, well I'll try not to, long story short I'm helping my sister with her passion. She started a business, so as family we are all helping as much as possible.

I feel like our relationship is suffering due to a lot of business-related issues, so I think it's healthiest if I move on and follow my own passion. I watched you follow yours and it inspired me more than the other queens. You weren't afraid to throw shade but also help someone that needed it. So, I feel as though I can trust your advice, haha =P.

I'm trying to save and pay off debts with my partner at the moment. We want to try to get a house, even though we are at a very low bracket we are working hard to try to make it happen. The question is (maybe I took more than a shortcut there) do I continue on this path and help my sister run the business and attempt to go to college too and pay what we need to? Or should I do a course online that will give me the qualification I need and attempt to fast track my career? This would mean leaving my family member and that's my problem. This would also mean putting the saving and debts on hold to a point.

Boring problem I know!

> *Thank you,*
> *Chloé*

Chloé,

You are so right!! ☺ This IS a boring problem. In fact, I had to have an EMT come in and put me on life support just to get through the second paragraph. But now that my vitals are stabilized and I'm breathing on my own again, allow me to help.

For starters, unless you and your sister are conjoined twins, your life is your life and her life is her life. It's great that you decided to help her out in her business—but it's hard for me to give you sound business advice not knowing what the business is. Flower shop? Dry cleaners? Meth lab? If she's opened a mortuary, you could kill her and (a) keep all the money for yourself, and (b) take her death, funeral, and investigation as write-offs!

I digress. If you and your "partner" are close enough that you want to buy a house together, then your loyalty should lie with her. (Loyalty ALWAYS lies with anyone who lies on top of you.) My advice is to find a way to ease yourself out of your sister's business and move forward with your puss-lappin' pal. Remember: You can always find another sister, but a good *scissor* sister is hard to find.

β

Dear Bianca,

I work in a rather casual office, where there is no actual boss; it's kind of a co-op arrangement. One of my co-workers is loud, obnoxious and constantly interrupting everybody. At least five of us have spoken to him privately about his behavior, but nothing has changed. He remains loud, rude and without boundaries. Any suggestions?

Craig
Savannah, Georgia

Dear Craig,

THIS is why socialism doesn't work. Fuck Bernie Sanders and fuck Jill Stein. If Susan Sarandon and all of her bullshit idealistic asshole friends had voted for Hillary, none of this would be happening. Socialism is like bisexuality—good in theory, but when the fuck has it really worked out?

Oh, wait, I'm off point. I think when you said "co-op kind of thing," I flashed back to my days working on a kibbutz as a small Israeli girl, where everybody worked and worked and worked and even the laziest among us got the same amount of money and food as the hardest workers. Oh, wait, I stand corrected. I was the laziest among us; so I guess socialism worked just fine. Oops! Feel the Bern!

Regarding YOUR problem (although I was enjoying talking about me), how about a little good, old-fashioned public shaming? Fuck this "talking to him privately" shit. Humiliate the jerk. Next time he bullies his way into a convo, just yell out, "Shut the fuck up, you bloated, AIDS-riddled loser!" (Admittedly, I have no idea what he looks like, or his health status, but it doesn't matter. Just saying it will make him a bit of a pariah—especially since you're in conservative Georgia, where "learning" is a four-letter word. Really, it is; in local textbooks they spell it "larn," which explains a lot about the state of your state.) No one will want to work with him!

If that doesn't work, you should go all Mean Girl on him. Every time he walks into the room, you should all huddle together and whisper and point and giggle. And if THAT doesn't work, well then, quit this bullshit gig and go find a job working with normal, non-granola-eating, non-co-op-y, gluten-addicted bottom feeders who have healthy senses of greed, selfishness, and materialism. Like me.

Ever done drag?

Dear Bianca,

There's no easy way to say this, so I'll just put it out there, and hope you don't throw shade. I'm in love with my boyfriend's brother and want to hook up with him. Okay, backstory: My BF Jake and I are both 22. His brother, Noah, is 19, and he's spending a month with us on his break from college. Jake is smart and funny and cute and I love him, but Noah has six-pack abs and a dick of death. Can I have it all without ruining my relationship with Jake? If anyone has the answer it would be you—you survived Drag Race and had it all.

Aaron

San Diego, California

Dear Aaron,

HAD it all is right. I went through that money faster than Kevin Spacey goes through Prep. Aaron, why would I throw shade . . . you whiny, selfish, covetous, home-wrecking piece of shit? Just kidding, Mary; I have no idea if you're whiny. But I do know that you need to get your priorities straight. A good boyfriend is hard to find, but finding a ten-inch dick is even harder. So, pack your bags, call an Uber, and let Noah matriculate in the back of your throat. **OR, IN BIG, BOLD CAPS**, see if Jake and Noah are interested in having a family "get-together." (You know what they say: "Vice is nice, but incest is best.") And if that *All in the Family* three-way works out, then you should all pack your bags, get plane tickets, and move to West Virginia, where "families like yers dun be the norm, nobody dun never marry anyone but kinfolk." Yee-hah! #DickPicsPlease #Deliverance #Banjo ☺

———

Bianca,

I'm a Democrat and my husband is a Republican. We've always enjoyed good political discussions, but ever since Donald Trump became president that's changed. We've agreed to no longer discuss politics or the news, but the underlying tension is beginning to take a toll on our marriage. What do you suggest?

Linda
Mission Viejo, California

Linda,

Most advice columnists would say that you and your hubby should go to a marriage counselor. But I'm not most advice columnists. I say, kill him in his sleep. Why spend all that time and money on a lost cause? A pillow over the face for eight and a half minutes, gentle pressure, will do the job. No marks, no bruises, no petechial hemorrhaging; it will look like he died in his sleep. Crib death for a grown-up! Then you'll be free to marry a Democrat. You're welcome.

———

Dear Bianca:

One of my sisters has a dog I hate. It's one of those yippy little Maltese-Yorkie-Shitzu-Cockapoo things. Problem is, my sister brings the dog everywhere, because she's a depressive and "Happy" is a therapy dog. We're having a big family event at my house and I don't want the dog there. Happy begs for food, barks, whines and pees all over the floor. How can I tell my sister to leave the dog at home without upsetting her?

Devon
Winsted, Connecticut

Dear Devon,

1. Your sister's dog, Happy, sounds just like my grandmother Hannah. We've learned to leave Nana Hannah in the garage when we have family gatherings.
2. Explain that her therapy dog is driving you into therapy. Be gentle and loving; maybe say something like, "Yo, sis. Leave Cujo at home or I'll put him in the fucking oven."
3. Tell her how you feel and understand that she might not come to the party. On the bright side, maybe your comments will trigger her depression, and she'll off herself, in which case you'll never have to deal with this problem again! Suicide is ALWAYS an option.

———

Dear Bianca,

My fourteen-year-old daughter has her first boyfriend, one of her classmates. He's a nice kid, but a typical fourteen-year-old boy—he plays video games, hangs with his friends, etc. My daughter is constantly upset and hysterical that he doesn't call every day and make her the focus of his life. I've explained that this is how boys at that age behave, but she's unable to hear me and she's becoming obsessive and depressed. Your thoughts?

Marsha
Doylestown, Pennsylvania

Dear Marsha,

First, I love that you spell your name "Marsha," not "Marcia," like Marcia Cross, that pretentious hag from *Desperate Housewives*. If you think I'm wrong about her, last time I checked she was "selling" shoes (on commission!) in an outlet mall in Pacoima.

Anyway, it sounds like your daughter is one step away from *Fatal Attraction*-like behavior. If so, hide your pet rabbit. You're right, the boy IS acting like a typical fourteen-year-old middle school rat. Your daughter, however, is acting like a middle-aged woman whose first two husbands went to the store for milk and never came back. No offense. I'm no doctor, but she sounds like a demanding cunt. She needs to try some therapy ASAP to nip this problem in the bud. Or, she needs to try lesbianism. Those girls are obsessed with obsession—and I don't mean the fragrance (which you can buy from Marcia Cross at the mall). A lesbian girlfriend will call her eleven times a day, sit in her truck outside the house for hours on end, and move in by Tuesday . . . with a cat or two, or six.

Problem solved, MARSHA?

xoxo

To learn etiquette, is actually learning how to see others, and respect them.

YIXING ZHANG

Yo, Hop Sing! I'd like a beef and broccoli with brown rice. And don't be chintzy with the soy sauce.

BIANCA DEL RIO

CHAPTER 6

CHEW WITH YOUR LEGS CLOSED

You should see
the nail gun I use
to hide my dick.

Fuck Black Lives; MANNERS matter. I'm a stickler for manners. Always have been, always will be. As far back as I can remember, I knew that elegance, propriety, and manners were important. First time I gave a hummer in a Walmart changing room I knew enough to keep Kleenex in my bra and floss in my jockstrap. Even then, I was a fuckin' lady. But I'm not the only one who cares about which fork to use, or which homeless people to help and which ones to step over. (I give money to the ones who make an effort—you know, the ones who decorate their cardboard boxes or pretty up their stoops. The homeless have nothing but time on their hands; they don't have to pick up dry cleaning on their way home from work, or get ready for a night at the theater—a night in front of the theater, maybe, but not IN. My point is, if they can't find twenty minutes in their "busy day" to hose down their bench or hang a couple of flowers on their shopping cart, why should I waste my time enabling such laziness? Tough love, my friends!)

Turns out, you get mad about manners, too. Lots of you.

Bianca,

How do I decline people's invitations without having any real reason to decline? You know what I'm talking about: someone invites you out to dinner but you just don't feel like getting out of bed! Any advice?

Amanda

Dear Amanda,

I think Nancy Reagan said it best: "Ronnie, get away from me with that old, withered dick!" Oh, wait, I'm sorry, she said, "Just say 'No!'"

You don't have to give a reason to decline. "No" is a complete sentence (as is "fuck you," "suck my dick," and "I hope you get hit by a car"). Give yourself permission to turn down the invite. However, if rigorous honesty makes you uncomfortable, then by all means lie. My personal favorite is "I'd like to go, but I have leukemia. Maybe next time (cough, cough)." No one will be mad that you couldn't attend. (Of course, explaining how the leukemia miraculously went away twenty-four hours later might be tricky, but you didn't ask me about that. I also don't want to answer because "technically" I'm not a doctor.)

———

Hi Bianca!

I am a bi woman. That's not my problem, but it has brought about several problems.

My issue is that while straight boys tend to be really stupid and gross about my sexuality (saying shit like "That's hot. Can I watch you with a girl hurr durr hurrrrrr"), lesbians tend to be flat out offensive.

I've had lesbians tell me that they won't date a bi girl because we're "more likely to cheat." I've also heard horror stories from bi friends who say that lesbians consider them "mopeds," meaning she's fun to ride, but she didn't want her friends to know she had one.

My question is, how can we on the LGBTQIA+ spectrum stop our own in-fighting and internalized prejudices, and unite to make life better for us all? What's a good comeback for lesbians who say this shit to bi women?

Hugs and slutty bisexual kisses,
Lulu

Dear Lulu,

Before I offer up my pearls of wisdom to solve your problem, I have to say, LGBTQIA? What the fuck is that? I understand LGB. I was even okay when they added the *T*, although to be perfectly honest I don't want to be in any group that counts Caitlin Jenner as a member. (I don't get her at all. He becomes a she, yet says she still likes women, but she isn't a lesbian. Huh? Now that Caitlin's a woman, shouldn't she be more like the other Jenner/Kardashian girls—addicted to black cock?) And I have no idea what the *I* and the *A* stand for. At this point you're just hoarding letters, like Vanna White on a three-day meth run. Maybe you should add an *H* for Hoarders. What's next, adding letters for some straight guy who got drunk and blew a sailor in an alley? That would make it LGBTQIAHSGGDABASIAA. Definitely won't fit on a protest sign at one of those annoying Lilith Fair festivals.

A lot of people don't understand the bi thing. That's their problem, not yours. Next time a straight guy asks if he can watch you and your girlfriend, you should say, "Sure, can I watch your mother and the cafeteria lady she's been fingering since you were in seventh grade?" And if a lesbian gives you shit, you can say, "Not Your Twat, Sasquatch. I wouldn't go down on you if you were hiding diamonds in your pussy."

So go be your fabulous bi self, and have a finger-lickin' good time! ☺

———————

Dear Bianca:

I'm happily married to my husband Jack, for 22 years, but he has one habit that drives me crazy. Whenever we're out at a restaurant or theater, he refers to the female staff members (waitresses, ushers, managers, etc.) as "honey," or "sweetheart," or "babe." I find it sexist and creepy and embarrassing. I've told him it bothers me, but he says, "They like it; it makes 'em feel appreciated." How do I get him to listen to me, and stop doing it?

Adele
Toms River, New Jersey

Dear Adele,

This is easy! When you go out, start calling all of the male staff members (waiters, valets, bellmen) "Handsome," "Hotcakes," or "Horsecock." I'm pretty sure Jack will get the message.

———

Dear Bianca,

I work for a very-diverse, multi-cultural company. They're holding a big costume party this fall. Last year, a Kenyan friend of mine gave me a traditional African dashiki as a gift. Can I wear it to the costume party or would that be considered offensive?

Jamie

Dear Jamie,

Everything is considered offensive these days, so who gives a fuck? I am soooooooo tired of people's "feelings being hurt" or their boundaries "violated." You want hurt feelings and boundaries violated? How about I shove your mother's dildo up your ass without lube? Two birds, one stone. Sweetheart, wear whatever the fuck you want. If you really want to be edgy, wear a torn, bloody dashiki, and go as a Ugandan citizen that Idi Amin tried to eat for lunch. In hindsight, perhaps I'm not the person to ask about propriety, since I'm on my way to blow Harvey Weinstein for a small part in his next movie and a pack of smokes—and I'm wearing Monica Lewinsky's jizz-stained blue dress.

Dear Bianca,

Our daughter Debra is engaged to a wonderful man. He's smart, he's successful, he's kind and he adores her. The only problem is that he has the world's worst table manners. He eats like a hostage who's just been released from captivity in an Ethiopian sweat lodge.

He slurps, he dribbles, he smacks his lips, he chews with his mouth open. He sprays food all over the table. It's disgusting. The only thing worse than having him for dinner in our home is having dinner with him in a restaurant. It's embarrassing. People stare, customers switch tables; the busboys sneak back over the border to Mexico. Is there anything we can say or do? Our daughter says nothing.

Angie
San Diego, California

Dear Angie,

Short of wearing sound-deafening headphones (like the runway workers who help land planes) or throwing salt in your eyes, there's probably not much you can do to make Pete the Pig clean up his act. He's a grown man, successful in every other facet of life, so you may just have to grin, bear it, and vomit in your mouth.

On the bright side, if that's how he eats his food, imagine how he eats your Debra! It must be a glorious mess. I'll bet the wet spot is so big it looks like Hurricane Harvey flooded the bedroom! No wonder she's silent at suppertime; she's saving her energy for screaming in the sack. By the way, this is the grossest question I've ever received.

Dear Bianca,

Last week, my friends and I (there were 5 of us) went to a restaurant for dinner. We were lingering after dessert and the manager came over, pointed to a long line of people waiting and politely told us he needed the table. We left but we were upset, and on the way out I gave the manager a piece of my mind. Was I wrong? Should I go back and apologize to the manager?

> _Betty_
> _Chicago, Illinois_

Dear Betty,

Unless you and your friends are blind you could clearly see a LONG line of people waiting for a table, so yes, you were wrong. You say you were "lingering after dessert," which means the meal was over. You paid for a meal, not a weekend stay. You could very easily have continued chatting in the parking lot, or a Starbucks, or a busy truck stop (where you could have picked up a couple bucks at the same time). I wouldn't make a special trip to the restaurant to say you're sorry, but next time you're there, you can take the manager aside and apologize, and explain you were stressed out because you were trying to decide whether to donate a kidney to your sick nephew, or sell it to him.

Dear Bianca,

As a female I never wear pantyhose, but I wonder if you have trouble getting dick-cheese out of your pantyhose at night?

> _Lily_
> _Denver, Colorado_

Dear Lily,

Of course not, silly girl! I keep my hose in the fridge, and in the morning I spread it on a cracker. Everything's better on a Ritz! I must say, Lily, this is one of the weirdest questions I've been asked. What are you smoking? Certainly not an uncut dick!

Dear Bianca,

I've been asked to throw a wedding shower for my friend LuAnn, who's getting married. For the FIFTH time. Is it even appropriate to have a shower for a woman who's been married so many times before? If so, what are the protocols? Please help ASAP; I have to let her know if I can do this.

Verna
Paducah, Kentucky

Dear Verna,

Fifth wedding? She must be running out of cousins! (I don't know if the clichéd "marrying your kinfolk" thing is really true. I've only been to Kentucky once: I went to the Derby and had a fabulous fling with one of the riders. Got me a little jockey-cocky; and if I say so myself, Señor Velasquez was hung like a horse! I don't mean his dick was huge. I mean it was brown and dirty.)

Anyway, yes, you can throw a shower for a fifth wedding, but I'd keep it simple. For example, instead of having it in your house or a restaurant, hold it in the office of Paducah's best divorce lawyer. It's not like LuAnn (a) hasn't been there before, or (b) won't be back. And in terms of gifts, make sure they're returnable and don't buy anything on layaway. Might I suggest some lovely Hers & Whoever towels?

Dear Bianca:

I lost my leg above the knee a few years ago due to a vascular disorder. I'm tired of explaining to people what happened. Is there a polite way of answering their questions about my leg?

Angelo

Dallas, Texas

Dear Hopalong,

I once had sex with an amputee. Yes, that's right, I humped a stump. And it was fabulous! He was a below-the-knee amputee; the only problem came when I was going down on him. He had taken the protective sock off his half leg, and out of the corner of my eye I could see his stump wiggling back and forth. VERY distracting. I said, "Yo, Bouncy, put the sock back on. My head's going up and down and your stump is going left and right; I'm getting vertigo!"

I don't mention this in a vain, braggadocious, "Oh, look at me, I'm so wonderful, I blew a cripple" kind of way. I mention it because it relates to your question. I knew enough NOT to ask Stumparella how he lost his leg; I figured if he wanted me to know, he'd tell me. I was more interested in what he did with the leg after the doctors took it off. Did he throw it out? Did he chop it up and turn it into mulch or plant food? Did he take it home with him and make it into a desk lamp, or cut it into pieces and make cute little nesting tables? (FYI, he never actually told me what he did with the leg, but on my way out of his house I figured it out. First time I'd ever seen a mailbox with toes.)

In my professional opinion, when someone asks, "What happened to your leg?" it's simplest to say, "I'm a pirate!"

Hope that helps, Angelo. Have a blessed day! ☺

P.S. Look at the bright side: you must save a fortune on shoes . . . shoe . . . you know what I mean.

Bianca,

My boyfriend and I are getting married. We're planning a small wedding (50 people at most) at a nice hotel. My BF John's parents will be there, but mine won't. My mother is VERY Christian (and VERY anti-gay) and refuses to attend. My father likes my fiancé and wants to go, but my mother is pressuring him not to. My mother met my boyfriend only once, and was "polite," but refused to meet him again. This will be the most important day of my life and I want my mother there. What do I do?

John Smith

Asheville, North Carolina

Dear Steven,

Why the fuck would you want your mother there? She sounds hideous. A wedding is a celebration—who needs a Christian sourpuss in a Talbots dress and soft shoes, scowling in the corner? (You know, I think I just described myself.)

You've invited her, and she's declined. Move on. Her loss. If you can convince your father to "man up" and attend, that would be great. If not, at least you know he's in your corner, and is just caught between a rock and a harridan.

So go have a fabulous wedding, and don't give Mommie Dearest another thought. Maybe someday she'll come around, and maybe she won't. And maybe someday your father will leave her for the twenty-year-old male parking valet he blew in the coatroom at your wedding.

Best of luck! 😘

Muah!

P.S. If you decide you want to be cunty (and I hope you do; you are gay, after all. What's the point of being gay if you're going to be pleasant and bland?), I have an idea. Take out a huge full-page wedding announcement in your local Sunday paper. You know, the newspaper that your mother—and everyone in her church—reads.

How's this for a sample announcement?

WEDDING ANNOUNCEMENT

This past Sunday, John Smith and Steven Remsen were married at the Motel 6, on Route 58, near the gas station that was shut down because the owner was using the bathroom as a meth lab. Steven is the son of General Joseph Remsen, a retired five-star general in the U.S. Army, and Madeline Remsen, a special-ed teacher in a really bad neighborhood. They were proud to walk their son down the aisle.

John, who is a party bottom, is the son of Mr. Smith, who is an invertebrate, and Mrs. Smith, who likes to start drinking at five o'clock in the afternoon to dull the pain of her tedious, heterosexual life. They were NOT in attendance, because Mrs. Smith thinks she's Christian and just can't deal with homos (in the kind, loving way Jesus did).

Steven and John met in 2015, at an S&M bar called the Happy Fist. The couple plan on honeymooning in a seedy bathhouse on the outskirts of Raleigh.

———

Dear Bianca,

I go to a lot of outdoor concerts and fairs. I'm getting tired of smokers sitting down near me and lighting up. I not only find it disgusting, but it makes me sick. What can I do?

Betsy
Lexington, Kentucky

Dear Betsy,

Assuming that smoking is legal in these outdoor venues, you have a couple of options:

1. You can politely ask them to move.
2. You can get up and move.
3. You can play the "cancer card." Tell them you just finished chemo and you'd appreciate it if they'd put their cigs out. (If not, throw on a turban. No one would ever believe you're driving a cab because you're white. How do I know you're white? Your name is Betsy, that's how.)
4. You can stay home and become a shut-in. Have your food and diapers delivered to the house, and catch up on concerts when the artists appear on PBS hustling their albums.
5. Tell the smokers that you're a spitter, and hope that spitting doesn't bother them. Every time they light up and blow smoke your way, you cough up a loogie and send it their way.
6. Eat a can of beans before you go to the concert. NO ONE will want to sit near you.

Xoxo
BDR

————————

Dear Bianca,

When at a dinner party in a restaurant, is it okay to start eating before everyone else is served, especially if the host says it is okay? I did this and my wife said I was terribly rude.

Dave
Chicago, Illinois

Bitch was wearing flats.
She deserved to die.

O. J.'s going to help
me find the real killer.

Great apartment
just opened up in
the building!

Nothing can ruin
my day when I
look good.

Dear Dave,

Your wife is right, although she's overreacting. Yes, you should have waited until everyone was served (unless of course you're on lifesaving medications that can't be taken on an empty stomach). But terribly rude? No. I once took a shit on the hors d'oeuvres tray, and blew my load in a napkin while a child was making a toast. THAT was terribly rude. What you did was just "normal rude." TRUST ME.

———

Dear Bianca,

This one time I was driving my car through the city and I stop at a red light that was about to change, so this kid was walking with his bike next to him, looks at me like he's better than everybody and takes a long ass time to finally start walking. The thing is that I couldn't take the fact that he was basically making fun of me so I hit the back wheel of his bike with my car, making him fall to the ground in a car safe area. My question is … was he coming for me? And was I wrong to do what I did?

Juan Gonzalez
Miami Beach, Florida

Dear Juan Gonzalez,

At exactly what point in time does a stolen vehicle become "your car"? I'm asking because in my country, possession is nine-tenths of the law, and I'd hate to see you get deported for boosting a Volvo. So if you've had it for enough time, no charges will be filed. I know, "whew," right, amigo?

As for the guy on the bike … how do you know he was making fun of you? Maybe he has a social anxiety disorder and he looks at everybody like that. Since you don't know, in that regard, you're wrong. But as for the taking his sweet fucked-up time crossing the street? HUGE pain in the ass. Probably not enough to warrant running him over, but certainly worth rolling down the window and yelling, "Yo, douchebag! Make a fucking effort!" Or however it is you say it in Mexican.

Since you're not likely to run into him again (either figuratively or physically), you should make what my AA friends (okay, friend) call a living amend: vow not to hit anyone else with your car over a minor annoyance. Major stuff, however? Pedal to the metal! VROOOM! *¡Me gusta!*

P.S. I'm guessing English is your third or fourth language, *si*? El buildo that wall-o.

———

Bianca:

I've been invited to my 50th high school reunion and I don't know if I should go. I hated high school. I was picked on and bullied for being gay (even though I wasn't out) and lived in constant fear. I've done very well financially (multi-millionaire) and both my husband and I are in great shape and look good. What do I do?

Mickey
Michigan

Dear Mickey,

MULTI-millionaire with a handsome husband? You GOGOGO to the reunion and you flaunt every fucking dime you have. Arrive in a private jet; take a limousine; wear designer suits and bespoke jewelry. Drop as many names as you can. Make sure you sit at the table with the biggest bullies. And THEN WINK AND SASHAY OUT THE DOOR AND SAY, "You know, if you boys had learned to take a load in the face, you could be living like this, too."

Dear Bianca,

I've been invited to a wedding. The invitation says, in bold font, **NO GIFTS**. *I'm not sure what to do. Should I bring a gift anyway, in case other people do, so I don't look like a cheap fuck? Or should I assume they meant what they said and honor their request?*

Help!

Dave

Denver, Colorado

Dear Dave,

Of course some douchebag is going to bring a gift. If he's the only one who does, then he'll look like an asshole. But he won't be the only one, and if a number of people bring gifts, then yes, you might look like a cheap fuck.

I'm not sure if, when people say "no gifts," they really mean it. I've thrown MILLIONS of dinners and parties, and EVERYONE knows I expect gifts. Nice gifts, none of that Hobby Lobby Popsicle-stick, potpourri bullshit.

My suggestion is to make a donation to a charity in the host's name. Can't go wrong. A lot of people donate to the Red Cross, or Meals on Wheels, so I think you should do something different, something special. Send a check to MY favorite charity, the Bianca Fund. (It's like the Jimmy Fund, in Boston, except instead of the money going to annoying sick kids, it goes to me. Hey, it's a write-off!)

Dear Ms. Del Rio,

I find it very difficult to balance helping others and looking out for myself. I hate saying no when someone asks for my help, but it is adding a lot of unnecessary stress to my day. What is the best way to say no without seeming rude?

Yours,

Grace

Dear Grace,

Pretend you're deaf. And you're asking ME how not to be rude? You wasted a stamp, dunce.

Love you madly.

Xoxo

———————

Dear Bianca,

There are only 112 shopping days until Christmas, and my husband Ed and I want to get a head start on buying gifts. What is your gift-giving process? Any suggestions?

Donna Jean Smith

Olathe, Kansas

Donna Jean,

That's two questions, not one. I'm guessing that in Kansas you have a lot of time on your hands because there's nothing else to do, so you sit around the farmhouse husking something, thinking of questions to ask Bianca. And I couldn't be happier! It's great knowing that I have a fan base with the Children of the Corn, and I'll cheerfully answer all of them. ☺

Before I answer your questions, though, let me just remind you that there are only eighty-seven days to return gifts until Hanukkah (save those receipts!), and only eighty-nine looting days until Kwanzaa. I'm joking, of course, Donna Jean; there are no Jews or blacks in Kansas.

One of the best ways to start shopping is by process of elimination. First figure out who you MUST buy presents for (i.e., children, employers, the PR guy who keeps your name off Megan's List) and to whom you can get away with just sending a card. Then, think budget. Figure out how much you can spend in total, then start breaking it down, person by person, gift by gift. For example, I have to get my agent a gift, because without him, I wouldn't have money to buy gifts. And, unlike most agents, my agent is a good guy, so a simple gift card to the Bunny Ranch (and subsequent penicillin shots) won't work. I have to get him something nice. I'm thinking a new putter, or a PlayStation, or maybe a couple of good books he can read while he's in the slammer for skimming money from his clients.

Speaking of reading, I'm also guessing that buying books is not on the table, what with you being in Kansas and all. Last time I was in Wichita, I asked a woman where the nearest Barnes & Noble was. She told me, "Phoenix." Her husband then chirped, "This is Kansas; we don't read books, we burn 'em!" What a kidder.

My suggestion to you, Farm Girl, is to buy gifts that are specific to the person you're buying them for, without breaking the bank. For example, your neighbor Arlette Johnson, who has been stress-eating since her husband, Buck, fell off his Lawn Boy riding mower and was slowly, yet symmetrically, mulched to death. In her grief, the widow Johnson has put on a little weight, say twenty, thirty . . . two hundred and forty pounds . . . I say, get her a gift certificate to Stuckey's all-you-can-eat buffet. It'll cost you a mere $19.99, but for her, it'll be a priceless gift, as well as a reminder that hubby number two should be a little less clumsy.

A LITTLE BIANCA

Since I'm now halfway up the ladder of success, I'm under pressure to be thoughtful. I ALWAYS have to send gifts and thank-you cards; I have to remember birthdays and anniversaries; I even had to send a thoughtful condolence to the widow of a man I hated. Even worse, I had to send a note to the widow of a man I jerked off in his car at one of his son's Little League games, while his wife (now his widow) thought he was getting some popcorn. It's exhausting.

Gift giving is a huge pain in the nuts, too, because the gifts have to be nice. Successful people know exactly how much thought and money went into buying their gifts. I can't just stop in some random Walmart and ask one of the hideously but appropriately low-paid employees to "pick out something really, really special. And keep it under eight bucks."

Things were much simpler in my old trailer-park days. Okay, I didn't ever really live in a trailer park, but for the purpose of this book, let's say I did. When I was invited for Sunday dinner at the Parkers' double-wide down the road—let's call it Lot #7, parcel #23—I didn't have to worry about sending flowers on Monday as a thank-you for the lovely repast of Tater Tots and Spam. The fact that I didn't fart at the table or wipe my hands on the dog was thanks enough for Mr. Parker and his wife/first cousin Lurlene.

Doing well is fabulous but grueling. As I become more and more famous, which God knows is as certain as Melissa Etheridge wearing her girlfriend as a hat, I'll have to figure out ways to handle the incredible yet exacting burdens of success. I think the first thing I need to do is make even more money so I can hire more "people." Then *they* can deal with buying gifts or telling my fans they're too ugly for me to take selfies with them.

I think the foremost quality—
there's no success without it—is
really loving what you do. If you
love it, you do it well, and there's
no success if you don't do well
what you're working at.

MALCOLM FORBES

Problem is, what I love to do is
illegal in forty-six states.

BIANCA DEL RIO

CHAPTER 7

WORK IT, GIRL!

When you go for a
job interview, always
put your best face
forward!

I got a gazillion questions about drag ... what do I do with my dick, what do I do with my balls, what do I do with the duct tape when I'm done, blah, blah, blah ... And by the way, "gazillion" means "any more than one" when it comes to questions about drag. And since drag is my career (I flunked out of both medical AND veterinary schools; I got drunk one night and spayed my teacher and gave a brow lift to a schnauzer), I put all "work-related" questions into this chapter. So, enjoy. Or don't. You already bought the book; I don't care.

Dear Bianca Del Rio,

My boss is a real asshole. He shouts and throws things when things don't go his way. He constantly tells his employees they are lucky to work for him even though he pays terribly. How do I stick up for myself against his constant abuse?

Thanks,
Charlotte Furneaux

Charlotte,

Charlotte? I'm onto you, Kellyanne! The White House is no place for you. Quit and go work for someone else, someone more even-tempered and rational, like Kim Jong-un or Chris Christie or Osama bin Laden's catty nephew Jerry. Honestly, I'm surprised you lasted this long; your wrinkles are starting to look tired.

(Is there anyone among us who doesn't think Kellyanne Conway is actually a middle-aged pharmacist named Dave?)

Hey Bianca,

I am a straight male fan over here in the UK. Been a fan of yours since I saw you on RuPaul's Drag Race (my girlfriend and I LOVED Hurricane Bianca). Now, I can't pretend to know what struggles and pains LGBT+ individuals go through, as I simply didn't have to face those issues growing up. But my sister has recently come out of the closet. My first (and most important) question is, what is the best thing I can do to make her feel happy & loved? I've been treating her as I did before, acting like it's the same as me telling my parents I finally got a girlfriend—is this the right thing to do? The last thing I want is for her to feel uncomfortable in her own home :(

My second question is, I've struggled with confidence issues my whole life (it's practically a miracle I have a GF), what can I do to help channel my inner Bianca? How can I stop caring so much what other people think of me?

Thank you for your time!
Conor

Dear Conor,

Oh, you precious thing, you're not straight. Yes, you may have a girlfriend, and yes, you may have sex with her, but, Princess, you didn't go to Dr. Phil or Dr. Drew for advice, you came to me—a nasty queen who puts the *F* in bitchy. So, that bit of reality aside . . .

If you want your lesbo sister to feel good about coming out of the closet, buy her tools so she can build an armoire. Handiwork tends to calm those gals down. Someone told me they love "craftsmanship." I learned this the hard way. My first publicist was an angry lesbian who used to walk down the streets snarling at people. She was more of a bulldog than a bull dyke. I wanted to put one of those plastic cones around her head so she wouldn't bite passersby. To calm her down before press events, I'd give her little tasks to do—whittle a spoon, smelt some iron, put up drywall in the ladies' room . . . and it worked like a charm. Your sister will appreciate the support and LOVE the new Black & Decker power saw.

As for building your confidence, try building your muscles. Go to the gym. Eat kale. Take steroids. Looking like a behemoth instills inner confidence. If you don't believe me, ask Khloé Kardashian. She's like The Rock without the shrunken testicles and back acne. Khloé doesn't walk into a room; she WALKS into a room. She—and everyone else—knows she has the biggest dick in the building. So bulk up, Conor. Be like Khloé. You'll be teeming with confidence. And who knows, maybe you'll start sleeping with black guys. Oh, wait, I mean, girls. Sorry, I forgot you're straight. Your faggy letter confused me.

———

Dear Bianca,

I am 5 foot 11 inches. My whole life, my mom told me I was too tall to wear heels. As an act of rebellion, I found myself trying to wear heels in my early 20s. I felt like a literal giant as everyone was watching me stumble in heels. I just want to wear cute shoes! Do you think I should get over this weirdness about my height + heels, or just stop trying the heels?

Too Tall Tammy

Dear TTT,

Stop trying the heels?! NEVER! I'd rather cut off a minor limb than give up my stilettos. Try using a wheelchair. You won't be so tall and you can wear heels without having to worry about stumbling. You'll also get really great parking spots near the mall. So put on the heels and hunch your way to happiness!

BDR

———————

Hello Fab Queen Bianca!

I kind'a struggle with self-confidence issues since I can think back. I'm 20 now and for me it seems as every 20-year-old is more attractive and successful.

How do I become so smart, pretty and succesfull like you?

I really love and admire you as my role model.

I hope I get to see you sometime but sadly not today Satan!

Very warm greetings from Germany,
Michelle
Diese Nachricht wurde von meinem Android Mobiltelefon mit GMX Mail gesendet.

Dear Fräulein,

Danke schön for your letter! There are many ways to boost your self-confidence. First stop on the self-esteem train is to learn HOW to spell. Unless you have tits OUT TO HERE and the pussy of death, no man wants to date a dunce. For example, it's spelled "successful," not "succesfull," and if you're going to use "kinda" rather than "kind of," then you need to add an apostrophe. At the END of the word. If you improve your spelling and grammar, you'll feel much better about yourself. Kinda'.

As for how to become as pretty as me? Easy! Buy a cheap wig, some gaudy makeup, cartoon eyelashes, and shave your balls. Voilà!

Xoxo
Bianca

P.S. I don't know what your last sentence in German means, but I hope it has nothing to do with ovens or Zyklon B. Just sayin'.

Dear Bianca,

Your advice is so great and so helpful to so many people. Have you ever thought about becoming a teacher, and helping our children learn the ways of the world?

Sally

Marblehead, Massachusetts

Sally,

Thank you so much for your kind words. While I would love to work with children, ~~I'm not allowed within 1000 feet of a schoolyard~~ my schedule won't allow for such a commitment. But if you do want me as a festive clown (clowns are all the rage right now!), I'm available for children's parties, bar mitzvahs, and funerals.

Hi Bianca,

My name is Rossanna but you can call me Rose. I'm a nineteen-year-old Mexican girl and since I was a kid I knew I wanted to do something big! A few years ago I realized I wanted to have my own company—I want to do makeup! Beautiful vegan makeup for everyone to use! But I don't know where to start, I don't know anyone in that industry that could give me advice or someone who could support me with knowledge or money. Do you know how I could start?

Anyway, thanks for everything. You are an amazing human being ♥ ♥ ♥ ♥ *we love you*

CLOWN BURG

One of two restaurants named after me. The other one is The Cornhole.

Hola, Wetbacko!

My name is Bianca but you can call me ICE Officer del Rio! ¡Adios, muchacha! Shit, that wall ain't up yet?

I don't know shit about starting up a company, but I do have an idea for you that might be both lucrative AND socially responsible. (Which, I assume, you are, by your desire to make vegan makeup. But have you ever met a happy vegan? I think not. Just sayin'.) I suggest you create white pancake makeup for illegal immigrants. Start with yourself. Make yourself up to look white, white, white, and change your name from Rossanna to Debbie. Then walk around the streets of a border town wearing a "Make America Great Again" hat and mutter, "Build that wall! Build that wall!" No one will EVER think you're Mexican and you'll never be pulled over, hassled, or deported. Promote your success and then go door to door looking for illegals; there are at least eleven million customers waiting for you, right now! And since most of them don't have bank accounts, you can make it a cash business and you won't have to pay taxes! This is a financial win, as well as socially responsible—your amigos will be able to stay in the country, and President Trump will be thrilled to see all of those happy white people. Plus, lawns and gardens all across this great land of ours will still look good! ¡Gracias!

P.S. You missed a spot in the garden.

———

Bianca,

I'm having an existential crisis! Do I get a job and do the 9–5 rat race or pursue my passion for art?

Charleigh B
Kilbirnie, Scotland

Charleigh,

You live in Kilbirnie, Scotland, what difference does it make? And I don't say that in a totally bitchy way (on the Bitch Scale of one to Mariah Carey, this is a six). Kilbirnie is a charming, quiet little town; I spent a month there one day. The population of Kilbirnie is 7,500 people, give or take a few old crones and a coupla sheep. Location matters when deciding what you want to do with your life.

You don't say what kind of art you're passionate about, nor do you say if you're very good at it—which is also important when making career choices. For example, I'm passionate about music. I love love love to sing. Unfortunately, I'm tone-deaf and couldn't drive to a melody with a map. My auto-tune app told me to shut the fuck up. But if you ARE good at art, then figure out the best way to maximize your talent. If you're a painter but like to paint skyscrapers, then moving out of Kilbirnie is probably a good idea. However, if your specialty is painting people being bored to death, then stay put and whip out your brushes.

My advice is, for now, why not try both? Get a nine-to-five job and do your art in your free time. After you've put a bit of money away, quit whatever boring-as-fuck job you've taken and move to a bigger city, like Glasgow or Edinburgh, where you can pursue your creative dream. If you don't like that idea, then why not just forget about the job, forget about the art, and become a hooker? Money's good, overhead's low (mouthwash and condoms), and who knows, maybe someday you'll paint pictures of guys blowing their loads in truck stops or back alleys! You're gay, right? If not, my bad. (Women don't make art.)

Bianca,

I am nineteen years old and trying to figure out what to do with my life. What is the best approach to finding out your passion in life and how to go about fulfilling it?

Alex

Texas

Dear Alex,

I think your first passion should be grammar so you can learn to not go from first person to second person in one paragraph. Anyway, I had so much fun making *Hurricane Bianca*. Filmmaking is so much more complicated than television or live performance. When I'm doing a live show, I know the beginning, middle, and end because I wrote the fucking thing. Reality TV is not as "real" as it seems; it's very well structured and the scenes are all mapped out. Film is different because things are shot out of order, with lots of last-minute changes, and the star (me) has almost no say in how it turns out. A hundred hours of film has to be edited down into a hundred minutes of film, and the star (me) has no control over what the editors and director do, so it's a little daunting. But *Hurricane Bianca* turned out great, so it was worth all of the stress and anxiety.

Hope that helps your depression! (Notice I made this all about me? Take notes!)

Anyway, back to *you* and your "passion." Finding your passion is the easy part; fulfilling it is the hard part. For example, let's say your passion is nuclear physics . . . but you're a fucking idiot. The odds on your getting a job as a physicist are about as remote as Rosie O'Donnell getting semen stains on her sweatshirt, cargo pants, or the rest of her lesbian uniform. My advice: Make a list of three things you have a passion for and then figure out which one you could actually make a living doing. Who knows, maybe you'll be good at *two* of them and have a really fulfilling life. (Remember Monica Lewinsky, Bill Clinton's "attentive" intern . . . the fat one with the beret? Anyway, my point is that Monica had *three* passions—sucking cock, putting cigars up her pussy, and hiding under desks. Turns out, the lucky bitch was good at all three! Talk about fulfilling.)

———————

Hey Bianca!

I think you're fucking brilliant, I loved "Not Today Satan" (Adelaide, Australia, July 2016) and I look forward to hopefully seeing your next comedy tour. Love you!

I work in retail. Most of the customers I serve are grumpy old arseholes that completely disregard my humanity and in an indirect, suggestive way, basically tell me to go fuck myself; as if I were born to serve them and kiss their feet. How should I deal with them? Be passive aggressive, kill them with kindness? Help!

Also, my shifts are extremely boring. How can I can keep myself entertained?

Thanks,

Amy

Dear Sourpuss,

Thank you for calling me brilliant; I appreciate the compliment! And you, too, are brilliant. At least brilliant enough to know that offering me a shallow compliment would guarantee my including your letter in the book. (But don't feel too special. My book contract requires me to deliver fifty-two thousand words. No way was I

A dash of salt and a pinch of Clorox! You can eat AND cleanse, AT THE SAME TIME!

leaving you out. Ever. Ever ever ever ever ever ever ever ever ever ever. Did I mention that contractually I have to deliver fifty-two thousand words? To the publisher?)

Amy, you're a retail clerk, not a Doctor Without Borders. Shoppers don't care about your humanity; they care that you bring them nice, open-toed shoes to try on. The best way for you to deal with these people is to not deal with them. I suggest you quit and find a work environment that's more attuned to your antisocial personality. Maybe you could get a job in a morgue, or a school for the deaf, or perhaps the International Space Station.

FYI, I don't think an antisocial personality is a bad thing. But I don't work in HR, now, do I?

#FUCKTHATJOB#ITSONLYGONNAGETWORSENEARXMAS

———

Bianca,

I work in a small office with five other women. Our boss, a 47-year-old man, has made vulgar, suggestive, borderline harassing remarks to the other five women. I don't know what to do.

Nervous in Nebraska

Dear Nervous,

First thing in the morning, you should march into the boss's office and say, "What's the matter, am I not pretty enough? You've harassed every other woman in this office, but not me. What's wrong? And I can suck the headlights off a Camaro going 120 mph on a salt lick. I have feelings, dammit!"

And if that doesn't get Bill O'Reilly's attention, call me; I can put you in touch with Gloria Allred, the Cunt Whisperer.

Miss Bianca,

I work with a wonderful woman. Not only is she great at her job, but she's sweet and kind and thoughtful. She'd gladly give you the shirt off her back. But there is one problem, and it's a big one—her breath. It stinks! You can smell her 100 yards away. Her breath smells like an anchovy's vagina. She doesn't smoke or have cancer, her hygiene is fine. I'm pretty sure it's because she has rotten teeth and gums. (It's hereditary—I've met her parents and they look like jack-o'-lanterns that have been left out in the sun.) I've casually offered her mints, gum, candies, etc., but she always says no. I don't know what to do. Any ideas?

Gary

Palm Springs, California

Dear Gary,

There's nothing worse than bad breath. Okay, well, that's not actually true, there are a couple of things worse than bad breath: climate change, camel toes, and Lady Gaga's second album, for example. But bad breath is a definite boner killer.

Since Hallie Halitosis has said "no" to gum, mints, and candies, offer her Listerine, cough drops, or hydrochloric acid. If she turns them down, too, every time she wants to speak to you, strap on a gas mask before you engage her. Her feelings may be hurt, but better her feelings than your sinuses or lungs.

Bianca:

One of my colleagues at work, "Frankie," is under the impression that everyone—including me—is hitting on his wife. He's been getting

This is what
happened when
Trump deported the

loud and obnoxious and kind of menacing, and he's creating problems in the workplace. Two important things to note: 1. His brother owns the company, and 2. His wife is a pig. I don't want to lose my job, but the office environment is really becoming toxic. Any suggestions?

Phil
Monroeville, Pennsylvania

Phil,

How fat is she? Can he have sex with her or does he need a Sherpa to mount Vesuvius?

First thing you might want to do is buy Frankie some glasses. If wifey is as hideous as you suggest, maybe Frankie is blinded by the possibility of big bucks to be earned by Big Bertha. (Not for nothin', but have you ever seen a thin Bertha? I haven't. The few Berthas I've met were either circus material or too big to even go to the circus, let alone join the circus as a novelty act.)

Second thing is, you might want to find another job.

———

Dear Bianca,

I'm a professional singer/actor. I have a nice career—I regularly appear on television in guest roles, I get some supporting roles in films, and I have a strong following on the cabaret/supper club/ theater circuit. All is good.

I need some help in dealing with a friend—a BFF, actually. His name is Steven and he is lovely and sweet. The problem is that he considers himself to be in show business—and he's not. He hovers around the edges of the industry, getting an occasional low-budget cable show, or hosts an LGBT charity event, or sometimes does a show at a cabaret. He lives off of his rich boyfriend (who, thank God, adores him and takes care of him). The underlying problem is that Steven HAS NO TALENT. None. Zilch. Zero. Nada. The Kardashians are higher up on the talent food chain. He bills himself as a comedian/singer ... but he's not funny, he can't sing ... and everyone knows it, but him. (He's handsome and charming, but so is my plumber, and the butch dyke who walks my dogs.) Steven is sort of like Zelig, in that he manages to befriend a lot of famous people, and gets to mingle in their circles. Yet he ONLY talks about himself and his credits—in rooms full of people with actual credits and careers. Steven is becoming a laughing stock amongst people who are actually in the entertainment industry. When his name comes up in show biz circles, eyes roll, and people snicker and giggle. His lack of talent is well-known (again, by everyone but him). If he knew what people think of his "career," he'd be terribly hurt, but he's doing such damage to himself and his reputation, I feel that I have to say something. But what? HELP!

Eric D

Los Angeles, California

Dear Eric,

His real name's not Justin Bieber, is it? Only kidding; Justin isn't living off his pastor ... I mean, boyfriend.

What to do? Say something, bitch, that's what! If not to "help" Steven, then for the rest of us, who may be subjected to his tin ear, non-funny bone, and insecurity-driven ego. I spend half my day worrying about ISIS, the other half of it worrying about Mike Pence, and the third half worrying that the filler in my cheeks might slip and mix with the collagen in my lips, and I won't be able to give a halfway decent blow job.

You can try to direct Steven into other show-biz-related careers. You can say, "Hey, Nicky-no-talent, have you thought about producing? You have such amazing leadership skills," or "Hey, Carl Clueless, you blend in with stars so well; you'd be a GREAT event planner," or "Hey, Gary Going Nowhere, have you ever thought about getting a job as a drug rehab counselor?"

If such gentle prodding doesn't work, then it's time for tough love. Next time you're in a crowded public place (where he'll be less likely to cry, hit, or bite), pull him aside and say, "Steven, you know I love you, right?" (Pause.) "Well, you know what you're trying to do for a living? Stop trying. You stink. You have no talent, and you're making an ass out of yourself!" (Pause.) "Coffee?"

Dear Bianca,

I don't really need any advice I just want to know when you're putting out a clothing line?

> Maggie
> Somerset, UK

Maggie, darling,

I already have a clothing line. It's by Barnum & Bailey and can be purchased at any circus, carnival, or sideshow near you! Seriously, other than students at the School for the Blind, who do you think would buy my clothes? My designs are so loud that Marlee Matlin covers her ears when I walk by. That said, if I can get Ivanka and her dad to Make America Great Again by producing my dresses overseas, for a nickel a week (Asian kids work cheap), then maybe a clothing line IS something I should consider.

And by the way, Maggie, you do need advice. On how to respond to direct questions. I specifically asked for advice questions, didn't I? And you specifically didn't. Just sayin'.

Love you madly. Dumb cunt.

Xoxo ☺

———————————

Dear Bianca,

Our church is putting on its annual summer play. This year we're doing Auntie Mame, and I've got the lead role. Do you think I should use Rosalind Russell or Lucille Ball as the model for my character?

Pat

Omaha, Nebraska

Pat,

Thank you, thank you, thank you! I LOVE theater questions; right in my wheelhouse. It's like asking Kendall Jenner about STDs. I think it's great that your church is putting on *Auntie Mame*; either it's a very gay-friendly congregation or a very straight congregation with very gay priests. Either way, all good. You don't say if you're a man or a woman, or perhaps a schizophrenic (you said "our" church but yours is the only name on the letter), but gender matters. Women tend to be vainer than men—remember in the Lucille Ball version of *Mame*, Lucy always looked fuzzy on camera, like she had a load of Desi all over her face? That's because she was 138 years old, trying to play 60. Fuck putting gauze over the cameras, they shot Lucy through a woven army blanket. If you're a gay man, go with Rosalind Russell: the fabulousness should come easy. If you're a woman, go with Lucy and the army blankets. And if you're a straight man playing Mame, you ain't that straight. Trust me, sister, you'll be ass up on a Pride Parade float by late November.

Bianca,

If you could perform with anyone, dead or alive, who would it be?

Mike
Burbank, California

Mike,

When you say "perform," I assume you mean onstage, as in doing a show with a fellow semicelebrity—as opposed to performing a sex act in a sling chair in a dingy basement with a well-hung D-lister.

What's up with only one? I'm like Carnie Wilson at a buffet—I need more. What if I wanted to perform with the Village People? Do they count as one, or do I have to pick one individual Village Person? (I'd take the Indian; feathers bring out my eyes.) What if I want to perform with Adele? Does she count as one or two?

Anyway, there are three "artists" I'd love to perform with:

1. Michael Jackson: I've always wanted to see, up close, how he blended the black parts of his face with the white parts of his face and the cherry-red lips. Not to mention finding out how he kept the fake nose in place—tape, glue, string, jizz?

2. Donny and Marie: More for the backstage experience. (I find their act nauseating; if he's a little rock 'n' roll, I'm a little straight. And as for "Puppy Love," in Vegas it's a song; in West Virginia it's a way of life.) I want to see Donny's Mormon Magic underwear. Is it a onesie? Does it have buckles and snaps? Does it have a picture of Mitt Romney on the ball sack? And what about Marie? Does she wear magic underwear, or maybe just a magic bra or magic tampon? Plus, performing with them would be my first experience in front of a semi-live, lily-white,

heterosexual audience who are all dressed in cheap polyester suits and faux costume jewelry.

3. Midgets or dwarves: I'm sure that somewhere in this vast and beautiful country of ours, there is a stage-worthy midget act, thrilling audiences with songs like "Ain't No Mountain High Enough," "Tiny Dancer," "Itsy Bitsy Spider," and "Big Girls Don't Cry." They would be perfect costars for me. Why? Do the math: 1 bitter drag queen + 5 singing midgets = guaranteed appearance on *America's Got Talent*! And if one of the midgets is missing a limb or has a wandering lazy eye, it's a winner!

Before the PC police come after me for not saying "little people," please note I am NOT using the words *midget* and *dwarf* in a pejorative or disparaging way. In fact, it's quite the opposite—I LOVE midgets and dwarves. Especially dwarves. If you don't know the difference, midgets are small but all of their limbs and features are proportional; dwarves have small bodies, but oddly formed arms and legs and giant heads. FYI, I once almost had sex with a dwarf. We were getting busy when I said, "Would you like a little head?" He got all pissy and offended and stormed out of the gas-station bathroom. I was offering him a blow job but he misunderstood and thought I was making fun of him because he was only two feet six inches tall but wore a size 94XL hat. Whatever.

———

Dear Bianca,

I work in a small office and our desks/cubbies are all very close together. The guy who sits next to me, Bob, is nice but he coughs all the time. I don't think he's sick—it seems like more of a

I don't always sleep here. It's a time-share.

nervous tic. It's driving me crazy and distracting me from doing my job. Everyone in the office is aware of it, so it's not like I can switch desks with someone; no one would make the switch. What should I do?

Maureen
Huntington, New York

Dear Maureen,

Gently and lovingly say, "Hey, Bob—either get cancer or get Robitussin, but it's enough with the fucking coughing, already."

Let me know how that works out for you.

Muah!

———

Hi B,

What advice did Joan Rivers give you that you apply to your career or personal life?

Thanks!
Susan
Huntington Beach, California

Hi, S,

She told me never to write an advice book—no one would care and no one would buy it. But she's dead, so I wrote it and you bought it. Fuck her.

Actually, Joan was the greatest. She gave me three great pieces of advice:

1. Work hard.
2. Never take a vacation (they'll forget about you).
3. Use industrial gaffing tape to tape my dick to my ass so it doesn't slip out when I cross my legs. Apparently it happened to her, once. MAYBE TWICE.
4. Never go to a private clinic for an endoscopy. (I'm kidding, she didn't say that. I made that up. She was in a coma.)

———

Bianca,

How do you deal with rude employees at your workplace? There are these two older women that are just plain rude and constantly lie about doing certain jobs and of course I'm trying to play nice but I'm getting to the point that I just want to curse them out . . . please help me out on what to do or say . . .

Much love ♥
Javier Garcia

Dear Javier,

There's nothing to *say*, but here is something to *do*. Next time one of these bitches lies to you, pick up your bus tray full of dirty dishes and crack them over the head.

Much love to you, too!

P.S. FYI, the only rude employee at my place of work is me.

BIANCA'S TIPS:
HOW TO DRIVE COWORKERS AWAY

Eat smelly Indian food at your desk.

Read the Koran and look shifty.

Change your name to Mohammad El Achbar Mohammad.

Ask your office mates about flying lessons incessantly.

Leave personal salves and creams all over your desk.

Have a Photoshopped picture of you and Hitler on display.

Put an "I ♥ Kim Jong-un" bumper sticker on your car.

Don't brush your teeth.

Gargle with semen.

Make sure your clothes reek of cigarette smoke.

Make sure your clothes reek of cigar smoke.

Make sure your clothes reek of cancer.

Shit yourself.

Shit yourself loudly.

Shit yourself after a cabbage lunch.

Who am I kidding, shitting yourself always works.

Hi Bianca!

First, I would like to say thank you for your charisma, uniqueness, nerve and talent. You are my favorite queen and a daily inspiration.

My question is about a co-worker, who I really hate. I have to work by his side, so I have been polite to him since day one, but he misunderstood me and started to think that we are friends. How can I explain to him that we are only co-workers and I don't want to be his friend?

Thank you,
Best regards,
Michelle

P.S. I am from Brazil, please send us a kiss!

Dear Michelle,

Thank you for your kind words. Allow me to return the compliment. Thank YOU (and all of Brazil) for the waxings. If not for you and your countrymen, do you know how much hair I'd have in my mouth? Muah!

There's a reason I work alone and am not part of some double act, like Bianca & Marie, or the Captain and Bianca, or Bianca-N-Pepa.

Your situation is easy to fix. Just come in to work a few times with open sores on your hands or face. Friendly Frank won't want to pal around with you ever again! (How you get those sores is your business, but, girl, I have puh-lenty of suggestions.) 😉

*If this outfit
were any blacker,
Kim Kardashian
would fuck it.*

I've seen some very beautiful
drag queens.
BEBE NEUWIRTH

Thank you. And I hope your
glaucoma clears up soon.
BIANCA DEL RIO

I received A LOT of questions about the world of
drag. Some people wanted to know about my expe-
riences working as a drag queen; many others were
interested in starting a career in drag. A LOT of the
questions were similar—and by similar, I mean THE
SAME! BORING! Thank God I'm not a proctologist!
How many questions about poop or wearing brown
can one woman answer?

I love the high neck. I didn't have to wax my tits.

Dear Bianca,

I'm transitioning out of the Fashion Industry and becoming a Psychotherapist. I'm thinking about combining my two worlds by offering a new form of "Drag Therapy" in which my clients would dress up as different "personas" that would allow them to express various aspects of their personality that they might not know very well. As a Professional Drag Queen, do you think this would be a viable form of therapy?

Dario M

Dear Dario,

I have questions about your question. But before I start, this is 2018, not 1958; when you use the word *transitioning*, it means you're changing genders, not jobs. Leaving one career for another is not the same as cutting off your dick.

1. What if your patient is like Sybil and has twenty-three different personalities? Have you considered how extensive their wardrobes would have to be? All twenty-three personalities may not be the same gender, and will certainly not be the same size. What if one of them is a pasty white anorexic and another is a black big'un, like Precious? Maybe personality number five is a winter, but numbers seven to seventeen are summers, now what? The point I'm making here is that your patients will have to spend so much on outfits they won't have enough money to pay for therapy.

2. Have you thought about people other than your prospective patients; you know, everyday citizens like me and Jamie? WE have to look at your patients. Imagine the trauma WE'LL have to deal with if Two-Ton Tessie comes lumbering down the street in a halter and Daisy Dukes. That image will be seared in our minds forever. It's worse than catching your parents fucking.

3. You don't say why you are leaving the fashion industry. Is it your choice? Is it because you got tired of watching gay men help bulimic supermodels clean up their vomit? Do you suffer from chronic exhaustion trying to figure out what the fuck Karl Lagerfeld is saying? Or was it the industry's choice? Do you just really suck at your job?
4. What makes you think you'd be a good therapist? I make no pretensions that I'm qualified to give advice. I'm just a whore for money, so when the book publisher called . . .

Anyway, it sounds to me like you may need therapy yourself. Let's hope one of your personas isn't suicidal.

Have a happy day!

Xoxoxo

———————

Hey, Bianca,

My name is Eric and I am 13 years old and I live in Greenville, South Carolina. You inspire me like Jiggly, Valentina, Alyssa and Willam and I wanted to ask your opinion on me doing drag. I've wanted to try drag for a while and I also wanted to know if you would be my drag mother. (I hope you say yes!) My mother is okay with it.

Thank You! ♥

Dear Eric,

Don't do drag—it's a trap! I'm kidding. Baby drag! I LOVE IT! I am so proud of you (not to mention your mother) for knowing who you are and what you are at such a young age. Muah! #proudproudproud. But I'm not old enough to be your drag mother, ya little cunt.

Dear Bianca,

I've been doing drag for fun for a while, but I'd like to do it for a living. I'm getting good at it, and think I have a shot. Is it possible to make a good living doing drag?

Any suggestions would be great. Thx

Dee Licious
Austin, Texas

Dear Dee,

LOVE your drag name. You're off to a good start. How do you define *good living*? If you mean only having to share a bathroom with four other people who live on your floor, then yes you can. If you mean having a phone (and calling plan) in your own name, then you have to be different from the other drag queens; you have to have a hook. For example, I'm a stand-up comic; Coco Peru is theatrical; Lady Bunny is fat. RuPaul was the first DQ to cross into the mainstream. Divine ate shit. So find your hook. Maybe you could cut off a limb and be the "hopping" drag queen. Or how about tucking your dick OUTSIDE your dress, and be the Flashing Queen?

Let me know what you decide. Let me know how I can "help." But as a drag queen, I totally don't mean that. Bye, bitch. See ya at happy hour.

Love you!

Hey Bianca,

I'm a new queen and as a boy I have quite small lips. I know you aren't the queen of natural lips, but how do you overdraw them without them looking obviously fake?

Much love,
Colin
Sent from my iPhone

Colin,

I love that you wrote from your iPhone. This tells me that you're either a busy go-getter with no time to sit at a computer, or you're homeless, and you sucked a cock for a cheap burner phone. Regardless, what matters is that your first thought was to write to me for advice. I'm honored.

But your question is stupid. I have no advice for you. By the way, my lips are real. Ask your father.

———————

Dear Bianca,

I'm a drag queen (Becky D'Vich) and I wonder if you get nervous before getting onstage? If so, how do you cope to have successful shows?

Thanks,
Becky

Dear Becky,

Of course I get nervous before I go onstage; EVERY artist does. (And I say "artist" instead of "performer," because I'm a pretentious douche.) We all have different coping mechanisms to work through our nerves. Before going onstage Al Pacino paces back and forth for hours. Barbra Streisand throws boiling hot tea on the lighting director. And Meryl Streep masturbates to Holocaust pictures from Auschwitz. I have much easier ways to cope: I do it with yoga and meditation. And by "yoga and meditation," I mean "booze and pills." Try that. (FYI, I don't share.)

Dear Bianca,

I have cystic fibrosis and watching your "Bianca Hates You" series in the hospital caused me to laugh/cough so hard the nurses thought I was having a medical emergency. Can you recommend any drag queens that are medically safe for me to watch?

Tiffany
Cleveland, Ohio

Dear Tiffany,

Pandora Boxx. You won't laugh at all.

Bianca,

How do you hide your penis?

Curious George
Atlanta, Georgia

Dear George,

The same way Beyoncé straightens her hair—it's a process. I tie a string to the tip of my dick, stick it up the crack in my ass, drag it up behind my neck, and tuck it safely under my wig. On one occasion my balls popped out, and I was complimented on my million-dollar earrings.

#RossDressForLess

I think families should vacation together, and cruising is a wonderful option.

MARCIA GAY HARDEN

Cruising *is* a wonderful option. Sometimes I even do it at sea.

BIANCA DEL RIO

CHAPTER 8

HIT THE ROAD, BITCH!

The only thing worse than a drunk queen on vacation is a drunk queen on a plane going on vacation. I've ~~been~~ seen both. Read this chapter and you'll never leave your house again. Except, of course, to buy the sequel to this book.

Dear Bianca:

My wife and I (and our two kids) have been invited to our friends' destination wedding. We live in Ohio. The destination is Tahiti, which is close to someone else's budget, assuming that someone is Bill Gates or Warren Buffett. It would cost us almost fifteen thousand dollars to attend the wedding. Even if I could afford it, I wouldn't go—it seems awfully rude to ask people to spend that amount of money to attend the wedding. We're very close to this couple; what's the best way to handle this?

Don

Shaker Heights, Ohio

Dear Don,

Best way to handle it? How about "Tahiti? Are you crazy? We can barely afford Trenton, let alone the tropics. We'll send a blender—why don't you stick your coconuts in it, you nasty, racist white fucks"? #whitepeopleproblem

While it's impossible for us to know our friends and neighbors' exact financial status (although if the repo man is sleeping on their porch, or Dad is pimping out his daughters to Shriners, you know it's not good), most people wouldn't put their friends in a position of financial unease. Let's give your friends the benefit of the doubt: I don't really think they expect you to attend, they probably know you can't afford it (Shaker Heights is lovely, but it ain't Bel-Air) but wanted to invite you, lest your feelings be hurt. If this is the case, then send your regrets along with a nice, affordable gift—maybe a book on manners or the name of a good divorce lawyer. (Don't give me that "Oh, Bianca, how the fuck could you say that?" look. Fifty percent of marriages in the United States end in divorce. And not nearly enough end up in a tragic, yet not unexpected, homicide/suicide situation.)

If we don't give them the benefit of the doubt—and they're just spoiled, unaware a-holes—then revert back to my original advice: "Tahiti? Are you crazy? We can barely afford Trenton, let alone the tropics. We'll send a blender—why don't you stick your coconuts in it?" #whitepeopleproblemwhyyoutakingupspaceinmybook?

———

Dear Bianca:

My boyfriend and I just broke up. We own a time share together in Cabo. We don't want to sell it, but we don't want to be there at the same time, either. Advice?

Neil
Los Angeles, California

Dear Neil,

You really can't figure this out? The answer is so simple. Send your ex on a "fact-finding mission" to the Sinaloa Cartel. *Adiós, muchacho!*

Muah!

Xoxo

P.S. Watch *Forensic Files* for some pointers. Good luck!

Fuck Julie Andrews.
These hills ain't alive
out here. They're just
hot!

CAUTION
DO NOT PLAY IN, ON
OR AROUND OR OCCUPY
THIS CONTAINER FOR
ANY PURPOSE

CAUTION
CONTAINER MUST BE PLACED
ON HARD LEVEL SURFACE
— LOAD UNIFORMLY —

**Athens
Services**
Waste Collection · Recycling · Transfer · Disposal · Street Sweeping
888/336-6100

*Fuck the beach. I got a
nice tan without getting
sand in my ass. It's a
win-win! This is the
second-best vacation
ever! The first was the
week I spent in the back
of Ricky Martin's throat.*

TRAVEL PET PEEVES

WAITING FOR LUGGAGE AT THE AIRPORT. Because I'm a globe-hopping celebrity with fans all over the world, I spend more time in the air than Kim Kardashian's legs. One of the things that drives me crazy is waiting for luggage at the airport. It shouldn't take me longer to get my luggage at LAX than it did for me to fly there from New York. It's not like they didn't know (a) we were coming, and (b) we'd have luggage on board. Yet it always takes an hour for the bags to start coming down the chute (which, FYI, is also a euphemism for getting fucked by George Takei). WHY?

PEOPLE WHO HAVEN'T FIGURED OUT HOW TO GO THROUGH SECURITY EFFICIENTLY. 9/11 was over a decade ago, as was that jackass shoe bomber. Laptops out, shoes off, pockets empty. Those things are simpler than George W. Bush, yet half the people on the security lines seem puzzled. Figure it the fuck out.

BIG, FAT PEOPLE SITTING NEXT TO ME. If you need to ask for a seat-belt extender, you need to get up, get off, and ask for a bigger plane. And don't ask for a Coke Zero. You're fooling no one.

PEOPLE WHO TRAVEL WITH FAGGY LITTLE DOGS AS "COMPANION ANIMALS." If you're so emotionally fragile you can't travel without your teacup poodle, you need to drink a teacup full of oxy and stay home. I own a horse (not Sarah Jessica Parker, an actual horse), but do you want me to bring Seabiscuit on board as my "companion animal"? Didn't think so.

PEOPLE WHO THINK THE FLIGHT ATTENDANTS ARE WAITERS AND WAITRESSES. They're not. They have far more important things to do than bring you vodka. Like jerk me off in the bathroom after I've extinguished the cigarette I shouldn't have been smoking.

SITTING NEXT TO A RETARD. I know, I know: "Bianca, you're not supposed to say 'retard,' it's wrong." And it is wrong, but not because it's politically incorrect; but because it's comedically broad, and comedy is specific. Yet it's a much funnier word than most clinical specifics. For starters, most retards are happy. All the time. Ever see a Down syndrome kid in a bad mood? No. Never. The Downsies are always happy, happy, happy! It's exhausting. For me. Because it means I have to be nice for hours on end. How would it look if I acted cunty to a retard? Billy has the IQ of a cantaloupe and wears round shoes that lace up the sides, while I'm multilingual (I can swallow in five languages) and wearing spiked Jimmy Choos, yet I'm giving HIM shit? Even Cosby's lawyer couldn't fix that kind of a PR problem. Moral of the story: You don't really have to be nice; they'll smile anyway.

PEOPLE WHO TAKE UP PART OF MY ARMREST. Girl, I do not have the patience for a seat hog. Which is why I carry a staple gun in my purse. I'll give you two chances to move over, and that's it! You want the armrest so badly, you can have it. Permanently. *Ch-chink, cl-ink.* Now your flabby arm is stapled to the seat. Enjoy the peanuts, fuckface.

PEOPLE WHO TAKE FOREVER GETTING THEIR SHIT OUT OF THE OVERHEAD BIN AFTER WE LAND. Drives me nuts; we've been parked at the gate for twenty minutes and some fat trailer-park chick is still trying to pull her shopping bags down. Hurry up, honey! Swap meet closes at ten.

PEOPLE WHO USE THE BATHROOM ON THE PLANE without first warning everyone that they're members of the Power-Shit-of-the-Month Club and today is Cabbage Wednesday. On days when I fly, I have Imodium for breakfast, a butt plug for lunch (and by butt plug I mean an entire urinal cake), and I douche with Glade. Why? Because I'm considerate, that's why. And because I'm a fucking lady. Take note, bitches. #Pureclass

Dear Bianca,

I travel a lot for work (I'm a computer programmer) and I have the whole "airport thing" down to a science. So it drives me nuts when people aren't prepared. They can't find their passports, or they don't know the confirmation number, or they speak no known language and can't tell the counter person what they need. I've nearly missed three flights this month for reasons like this. What to do?

John
Denver, Colorado

Dear John Denver,

For starters, don't take a solo ride in a glider in the mountains. Oh, wait, you're John FROM Denver, not John Denver. My bad; color me embarrassed.

The quickest way to move a straggler on line in an airport is to yell out, "Hey, Slowpoke! I'm in a hurry. Hear that ticking? My vest is set to go off in five minutes. Shake a leg, will ya?"

After a brief stop with the good folks at the TSA, you'll be on board in no time!

And John, you ain't the only frequent flier who's fed the fuck up.

Dear Bianca,

My BF and I are going to Germany on vacation. He wants us to take a German language class so we can be conversationally fluent when we get there. I have no interest in taking the class, and we're fighting about it. Any advice?

Lisa
Monroeville, Pennsylvania

Most "outdoorsy"
types of gals are
lesbians. Not moi!

Dear Leisl (notice the Germanic twist I put on your name? How fabulous am I?),

If your BF wats to spreken zee Deutsch, let him. No need for you to take the classes. Not your monkey, not your Black Forest. I travel the world and I can barely speak English, and no one seems to care. As long as my dick stays taped to my butt and the jokes work, I'm as welcome as FEMA at an earthquake, or paper towels in Puerto Rico. (Google it.) There are only a few expressions you'll need to know to navigate your way around Germany (your linguist BF can do the rest of the talking):

Wo ist das Badezimmer?
Where is the bathroom?

Wo ist das beste bar?
Where is the best bar?

Ich bin verloren. Kaanst du mir helfen?
I'm lost. Can you help me?

Ich bin nicht Juden. Warem fragst du?
I'm not Jewish; why do you ask?*

*Then run for your life.

———————

Bianca,
I'm addicted to Discovery ID TV. Where would you hide a dead body?

                                        Casey
                                        Florida

Casey,

I'm very impressed that you're addicted to TV. Whitney Houston had a hole in her sinuses just from doing blow, yet you somehow manage to snort a fifty-two-inch LED flat screen without so much as a sneeze? You go, girl!

I've never killed anyone (certainly not with kindness) but it sounds like you're thinking about it. If so, can I give you a list of people to start with? I'm just kidding (I can hear my lawyers peeing themselves reading this) . . . but if I were to off somebody, disposal would depend on how I killed them, where I killed them, and who they were. Let's say, for example, that I shoved Martha Stewart into an oven and baked her to death (at 350 degrees for ninety minutes). When she came out of the oven she'd be so stiff from baking her—so I wouldn't have to dispose of the body. I could put an apron on her and leave her in the kitchen and people would think Martha was just being her usual self.

There are lots of good places to dispose of a dead body. For example, let's say you kill your baby daddy and you're a fan of *Fargo*. I say, "Time for the wood chipper!" This one's easy-peasy, because once you're done with the annoying gruesomeness and it's time for a BBQ, the baby back ribs might actually taste like your baby daddy's ribs! (And if the police want evidence, they can come back the next day and sift through your shit.)

If you need more information on body disposal, please check out my upcoming website, www.where'dthebitchgo?.com

I'm not interested
in fame, at all.

CRYSTAL REED

Who the fuck
is Crystal Reed?

BIANCA DEL RIO

CHAPTER 9

TMZ OR TMI?

*Every Tuesday night
dress like Evita and stand on
my balcony and sing. And every
Wednesday morning my doctor
comes to the hospital to get me out
of lockdown.*

On the celebrity food chain, I fall somewhere between Bethenny Frankel and the midget on *Game of Thrones*. For now, it's a good spot to be in. I'm famous enough that I can get good dinner reservations, cut lines at airports, and park in disabled parking spots (even though there's nothing fucking wrong with me. I don't limp, wobble, or drag a leg. Can you imagine walking a runway in stilettos with a deformed foot? EEEwwww!). The questions in this chapter are about fame, fortune, and *felching*. —Okay, okay, there are no questions about felching, but I wanted to make an alliteration and the word *felching* is so sadly underused in today's society I figured, "Why the fuck not?"

Dear Bianca,

Winning season six of RuPaul's Drag Race *has made you famous and successful. How has that changed your life?*

Andre D
Chicago, Illinois

Dear Andre,

First off, thank you for your predictable question. I've been asked this almost as often as I've been asked, "Is sperm fattening?" (No. If it were, Anderson Cooper would weigh six and a half tons.) Winning *RuPaul's Drag Race* changed my life. Success has turned me from a snarky, thirty-seven-year-old man who tucked his junk into a cheap dress and gave blow jobs in bathrooms into a snarky forty-two-year-old man who tucks his junk into a cheap dress and gives blow jobs in nice hotels.

Before I go further, have a cocktail, or a Xanax, or a line of whatever, because this is going to be a VERY long answer. And not because your question is so scintillating (YAWN!) but because it's about me. And success. Which go together like Michael Jackson's hand and a nine-year-old cock.

I remember the moment when RuPaul announced my name as *Drag Race* winner as though it was yesterday. Which it actually was, because I watch the fucking thing online, over and over and over again, every single day. Not because watching it makes me feel better about myself, but because it makes me feel better about all the bitter twats I left in my dust who now loathe and resent me and covet my things.

"And the winner of *RuPaul's Drag Race*, and America's Next Drag Superstar . . . and winner of $100,000 is . . . Bianca Del Rio." I collapsed in one of the runners-ups[*] arms, and while blinking frantically as my mind raced through all the ways I could spend the money, I accidentally knocked one of my fake eyelashes into my eye and began tearing up. Everyone thought I was overcome with emotion when in reality I had a slightly scratched cornea and a fabulous sense of false pride—which has served me well these past few years and made it easier for me to climb the ladder of success without having to claw my way over anyone standing in my way . . . unless I wanted to.

---

[*] "Runner-up" is a nice way of saying "loser." When is the last time you asked a child, "So, Little Billy, what do you want to be when you grow up?" and they answered, "Why, Miss Gibson, I'd like to be the first or second runner-up in some mindless pageant or shallow, empty contest."

I've always believed there were two kinds people in the world: 1. rich, successful people who had pretty clothes and nice things, and 2. people who resented them, otherwise known as everyone else. And I mean *everyone*; as much as I like Pope Francis for his kind heart and basic inclusiveness, I don't believe for a second that when the pontiff sees Donald Trump on TV he's not thinking, "Rich prick. All that money, fix your hair!"

Go get another cocktail, I'm not done yet.

Time to address the elephant in the middle of the room—and no, Adele's not here—I mean the age-old question: What exactly IS success? This question has been asked by generations of people for hundreds of years. A question asked almost as often as "What the fuck is it that the Kardashians DO?"

Of course, the people who ask this question are usually altruistic failures, trying to justify their lowly stations in life by bathing themselves in the notion of the greater good. For example, poets, philosophers, and lesbian do-gooders who have given up shaving, air conditioning, and Netflix to go live in African huts where they pick the nits off of bloated children and their constantly pregnant mothers. Those spiritual losers will tell you that success is not tied to the material things you have gathered in this world, but to the good things you have done to make this world a better place.[*] Even Einstein, the brainiac physicist, was not immune to such bullshit. He once said, "Try not to become a man of success, but rather try to become a man of value."

I know what you're thinking: "Einstein had a lot of value—he made

---

[*] FYI, not ALL disenfranchised people are kind and loving and looking out for others. When's the last time a homeless person stuck his head out of his box and offered to buy you a sandwich or a mocha latte Frappuccino? Fuck them. Just sayin'.

The Walk of Fame today, the Betty Ford Center tomorrow. A girl can dream.

Why wait?

huge contributions to the world with his work in quantum physics."
True. But do you know what *I'm* thinking? That Einstein had a credit
score of 240 and his hair was a fucking mess. That's what.

To any sane person (or mildly damaged person who's on the
right meds) success *does* involve having nice things. When I'm
on tour, going from city to city spreading the hate to people who
watched me on *Drag Race* (or people who didn't watch me on *Drag
Race* but just came to my show wondering if they could see my
dick through my dress), I've never once driven through a low-rent
slum and thought, "My God, I'll bet the good folks who live in these
bombed-out shacks are really successful motherfuckers." There's
nothing fabulous about not having money. Be honest—would you
rather live in a house overlooking the beach in Malibu, or on the
beach in Malibu looking up at a house?

I learned to have misguided values in spite of my parents' best
efforts to teach me otherwise. At a young age, sometime during my
formative wonder years (one to twenty-nine), my mother sat me
down and lovingly said, "Sweetheart, money can't buy happiness."
And I lovingly replied, "What the fuck is wrong with you? Of course it
can. And if it can't, I'd rather be miserable in Chanel than happy in
polyester." Even then I knew.

Now, please understand that I'm not rich . . . yet (I have plans) . . .
but I'm doing well enough that I no longer have to ask the waiter
if the salad is extra or if it comes with the meal. I have my people
ask that question for me. I no longer talk to the staff. Yes, I have
people. Okay, person—I have one people, but he does everything
for me. He answers my phones, checks my mail, manages my
calendar, and tells me at least five times a day (like a Muslim facing
Mecca to pray—which they do when they're not blowing shit up)
that I'm talented and fabulous and don't need to take selfies with
audience members who are ugly, fat, or in desperate need of a

depilatory or dermabrasion. By the way, I think everyone should have people—I mean underpaid sycophants who do everything for you while allowing you to berate and scold them, minimize their contributions, and cripple their self-esteem. If you think I'm kidding, there's a show-biz urban legend that on the original 1990s *Rosie O'Donnell Show* (when she was still the "Queen of Nice," as opposed to the 2018 Rosie, who presents as an angry lesbian with eight thousand children and severe control issues) one of the guests was the puppet Witchiepoo from H.R. Pufnstuf fame. Things were running late in New York that day when the head segment producer ran through the office looking for Rosie, yelling, "Everybody shut up! I have Witchiepoo's people on the phone!" The story goes that every staff member stopped whatever they were doing and began sobbing at the realization that they, college graduates, were toiling eighteen hours a day in windowless cubicles while a fictional cloth hand puppet had "people."

But success is not just about having money or people, it's also about being famous enough to get into clubs you could've previously never gotten into, even after you blew the owner, the doorman, the bouncer, and the bouncer's fat, "bi-curious" cousin, Lazy-eye Eddie. It's about being able to get out of traffic tickets or court appearances or hotel rooms with DNA evidence all over the bedspread.

In *Harry Potter and the Sorcerer's Stone*, J. K. Rowling wrote, "Tut, tut—fame clearly isn't everything." To which I say, "Really? Go tut-tut yourself." If Bill Cosby . . . I mean, DOCTOR Bill Cosby . . . was a fry cook, not a famous comic, I'm pretty sure he'd be serving hard time for his hard-ons . . . Hmm, if Cos did go to jail, I wonder if he'd make his cell mates call him Doctor?

Your password is frumpy, *now hurry the fuck up!*

Dear Bianca:

Being famous looks like so much fun—the parties, the clothes, the paparazzi. Are there any downsides to being famous?

Bobby J
Memphis

Dear Bobby,

Other than answering questions like this, NO! I'm just kidding, Bobby; there are plenty of downsides.

First is the "being nice thing." Wow. That is so not easy for me—hateful is my default mode. When I wake up in the morning, my first thought isn't "oh, what a beautiful day," it's "Jesus Christ, not again." I have to work at being nice, especially offstage. Being nice offstage is important to my business, because if I'm snarky when I'm out and about—shopping, loitering, having cocktails—it ruins the illusion I create onstage, and why should people pay for my sketchy attitude in a club or theater when they can get it for free by simply staring at me when I'm shoplifting at Talbots, or loudly saying "tsk tsk" when they see me roll my eyes at a blind beggar lying in front of a Ronald McDonald House. I can't be giving it away for free. Penn & Teller aren't walking through the mall magically pulling quarters out of kids' ears, are they?

Also, I'm not famous enough . . . yet (I have a plan) . . . to get away with being difficult offstage. I call this the "Katherine Heigl" effect. Here's a refresher: Katherine Heigl was in the original cast of *Grey's Anatomy*, the long-running TV show about doctors and interns who are way too young and pretty to be doing brain surgery or resecting bowels. After making a few movies, Katherine Heigl got confused and thought she was Katharine Hepburn and became all pissy and snotty and impossible. And suddenly she was no longer on *Grey's*

Anatomy, she was on food stamps. (Okay, I don't know for a fact that she was on food stamps, but I do know she wasn't on TV or anyone's radar.) She became the Helen Reddy of her generation. Don't know who Helen Reddy is? That's right, you don't. Here's why: Helen was an Australian pop singer who had a string of monster hit songs in the 1970s. She was all over the radio and the pop charts. Then she turned into a monster. And then she was just over. Last I heard, Helen was back in Australia, shearing sheep and trying to get people to recognize her. If you want to be a diva like Barbra Streisand, you have to have the talent of Barbra Streisand, and the only person with the talent of Barbra Streisand is Barbra Streisand. Babs has turned cunty into a cottage industry. Good for her.

Another downside of semifame is that everyone thinks you're rich, and they expect you to pay for everything. Which is bullshit, with a capital *F.* I'm not rich (although I'd like to think I'm richer than you—and you buying this book will help me get there), but even if I was, I wouldn't pick up every check, or treat all the time. And not as a matter of principle or fairness, or because I don't want to enable your codependency, but because I'm selfish. Look, you all know how much I care about you, and I do. But as much as I care about you, I care about me just a little bit more. So, with all due respect and lots of hugs, pay for your own fucking dinner.

The third biggest downside of success is that it's exhausting. You have to act successful ALL the time. At the store, at the restaurant, at the free clinic. You can never fuck up and be yourself and act like a turd, or you'll wind up at the unemployment office, on line next to David Caruso and Helen Reddy. I miss the old days when I could play "pull my finger" at a funeral and not worry about it winding up on TMZ later that night.

Hey,

First off, big fan! I think you may be my spirit animal.

I have a severe case of resting bitch face, and a lot of the time people think I am angry or I hate them… what advice would you give? Yours is glorious, might I add!! ♥ ♥

Roisin xx

Scotland

Dear Roisin,

I love that you started your letter with "Hey," like we're friends, or we have that kind of a relationship. Hahaha. We're not and we don't. Just kidding. You bought my book, of course we're friends. But I have no idea what a spirit animal is—I'm hoping you mean an epileptic with a horse dick. Think of the fun ride! And the endless teeth. You'll be like twins.

I think resting bitch face is an asset, not something to be changed or apologized for. Who needs perky and smiley 24/7? Uggh. Can you imagine being with Kelly Ripa for more than five minutes? … Really, Kelly Ripa for five minutes. Pull the trigger with your toe!

Don't apologize for or change your resting bitch face. In fact, I suggest you up the ante, and start developing a resting cunt face. If most people think you're angry or hate them, good! The people who understand resting bitch face are the only people worth hanging with anyway! Ask Faye Dunaway. I'm kidding, that's not her real face.

When you're paying for it, my favorite drink is all of them.

CELEBRITIES WHO ARE WAY TOO PERKY

KELLY RIPA: She makes Kathie Lee Gifford look like Sylvia Plath. She is way too bubbly for six in the morning. If I want bubbly at that hour, I'll crack open a bottle of Dom Pérignon.

ROBIN ROBERTS: A lesbian with cancer *and* a dead mother. And yet she's perky. What's up with that? I'm perfectly healthy and looking fab, and I'm not half as upbeat as she is. I don't get it. Maybe she eats Prozac for breakfast.

MARIO LOPEZ: Great guns, killer abs, big smile. Good marriage, healthy kids, great career in spite of no talent. I get it. He's happy. But the constant go-go-go perkiness? At some point he's just rubbing it in.

THE SLOPPY BLOND GIRL ON TMZ: I have no problem with her being happy. She gets paid to gossip about stars on TV all day long. But she's kind of a slob. I don't imagine she's got a hot boyfriend. So calm down, missy; things could be better.

RICHARD SIMMONS: Although the fitness guru has become a bit of a recluse (think Howard Hughes with better nails), on the rare occasions when he IS spied in public he is just as disturbingly bubbly and chipper as we remember. I'm just glad he got rid of the tiny striped shorts. Last thing I need to start my day is a ninety-year-old elf with his junk hanging out of his pants.

SHERYL UNDERWOOD: She is the fat, jolly black woman on *The Talk*, the type of fat, jolly black woman you only see on TV. Sheryl is playing her role on the show perfectly. She's upbeat, she's chirpy, and she's funny, in an "Mmhmm, girl" kind of way. I know she's making good money, which might explain some of the perkiness, but truth be told, Sheryl's cholesterol is probably higher than the ratings. Something tells me she won't be quite so perky in a mahogany box.

DOLLY PARTON: I LOVE Dolly Parton. She's as close to being a drag queen as a woman can get without having a strap-on or a dick. That said, forty years of clucking and giggling can get on your nerves. Is she NEVER sad? Is everything ALWAYS good, ALWAYS joyful? Be honest, just once, wouldn't you like to see Dolly sitting in the yard, barefoot, wearing a torn housedress and cheap lipstick, lighting up a smoke, and mumbling, "Daddy won't fuck me. Y'all know that, right?"

TOM CRUISE: He is a giant ball of WTF! He laughs ALL the time. From Oprah to Fallon to Colbert to Conan, whenever he sits down he starts laughing. Maybe he's got a fuzzy butt plug stuck in his perfectly round bubble ass. Tom doesn't just laugh at jokes, he laughs at greetings, and news items and commercial breaks. Clowns aren't that fucking happy. Yes, he's worth a gazillion dollars, and even at 105 years old he still has a killer smile, but seriously? Maybe page 55 of the Scientology manual says, "Smile and laugh, naturally. Turn to page 56."

Money can't buy happiness. But it can buy a week in Paris and a new vibrator.

If we lose love and
self-respect for each other,
this is how we die.

MAYA ANGELOU

Bitch died. See where
all that "respecting others"
bullshit got her?

BIANCA DEL RIO

CHAPTER 10

IT'S ALL ABOUT ME

GREENBLATT'S

*I wasn't hungry,
I just stopped in
to complain.*

You're probably thinking, "This will be my favorite chapter in the book because I SOOOOO love Bianca, I want to read and think ONLY about HER, all day and all night long, 24/7, 365 days a year!" While I'm flattered by your borderline stalk-ish admiration, you're wrong; this chapter is more of a potpourri than an homage to *moi*. And FYI, when I say "potpourri," I mean a hodgepodge of loose ends, not a bowl of scented leaves you put in the bathroom so the whole house doesn't stink when one of your fat friends comes over and takes a huge power shit in the sink. While some of the questions in this chapter are about me, the truth is I just got tired of writing this goddamned book and took whatever leftover letters I couldn't find a proper chapter for and shoved them in here. Okay???

Bianca,
    Have you gotten in touch with your inner child?
                                      James
                             Cleveland, Ohio

James,
    Yes, I have. Her name is JonBénet.
    James, I hate the expression *get in touch with your inner child*. It's more annoying than hearing dentures click when you're getting head. Jared from Subway was told to get in touch with his inner child—how'd that work out for

everybody? Okay, maybe Jared misunderstood, and thought it was "get inside a child," but still, I'm pretty sure the outcome would've been the same.

Even worse, what if your inner child is one of the Menéndez Brothers? Chances are the present-day you is far better than Lyle or Erik, so should you really be reaching back into your past to meet your younger self? I'll bet your parents would be none too pleased with this discovery.

The only way I'm okay with the "inner child" thing is if the inner child actually IS an inner child—you know, a fetus stuck inside a fetus during a freakish pregnancy. I see this sort of stuff all the time, usually on TLC or some random fetish website I *accidentally* came upon. Fetus number two starts out as a tooth with hair, but by the second trimester he's Little Jimmy, and now fetus number one is a baby daddy and the pregnant woman is going to be both a baby mama AND a baby grandmama. Fabulous, no?

Look, of course I want the tooth with hair to grow up and be pretty and healthy (I'm cunty, not cruel). I want ALL children, inner and outer, to come out in perfect health; I just don't want to hear about it, especially if the "inner child" belongs to a fifty-eight-year-old dermatologist from Queens trying to work out his "I could never please my daddy" issues, okay?

Oh, and one last thing, James. I don't understand men named James who insist on being called James. Pre-fucking-tentious. What's wrong with Jim, or Jimmy, or even, God help me, Jimbo? Unless you're famous like James Taylor or important like James Madison, insisting on being called "James" isn't cool, it's stupid. You don't see me using MY real name, do you? Of course not; I'm cool. (FYI, my real name is Shitface.) Thank you so much for your question. Hope I was helpful! 😊 😊

Dear Bianca,

If you were stuck in a lift (elevator) with Donald Trump, what would be your opening line?

Becki
London, UK

Becki,

"OMG, Donald Trump! Mr. President, can I just say, your son Barron can really suck a dick?" (Don't judge me; rich retards need love, too.) Of course, I may just vomit in my mouth and then feed it back to him, the way Alicia Silverstone feeds her kid.

Dear Bianca,

How much makeup is too much? My mother says when I put on lipstick or use blush, I look like a whore.

Mary
Swarthmore, Pennsylvania

Dear Mary,

Your mother's a cunt. Look at ME. Whore is my middle name.

P.S. I once knew a woman in Swarthmore, Pennsylvania. Snooty bitch, you couldn't drive a pin up her ass with a jackhammer. And I tried.

Bianca,

    Firstly, let me say that I'm a big fan of yours and someday I hope to meet you. Secondly, if (I mean, when!) that day comes, I don't want to offend you, so … do you like to be referred to as "she" or "he"?

Allan G
Wasilla, Alaska

Allan,

    Firstly, you can't offend me. Nothing offends me. I'm okay with kicking puppies and burning down nursing homes. Secondly, *firstly* is not a word. Thirdly, I look forward to meeting you someday, too. (Although, truth be told, until Sarah Palin and her kids Bristol, and Boo-Boo, and Trick or Treat move to Peru, there's not an Eskimo's chance I'll come to Alaska. Besides, you can't look fabulous in mukluks. And Mommy doesn't do ice.)

    Truth be told, what you call me depends on who you are. (Real answer.)

What does RuPaul smell like?

Gina
Brooklyn, New York

Gina,

    She smells like Lady Bunny's pussy.

Bianca,

How many pounds of makeup do you go through in a year to get that natural look?

Devon
Los Angeles, California

Devon,

I assume by "pounds" you mean "tons"? And by "natural" you mean "like a corpse"? (If I was your grandmother you'd say, "Oh, she looks so peaceful.") I obviously go through massive amounts of cheap makeup. When I leave Costco my cart is loaded up. I take more loads than a hooker in Las Vegas.

But none of my makeup goes to waste. In fact, I recycle! After a show, when the handlers and trainers come backstage to hose me down, I stand in a giant bucket so that when they turn the faucets on my makeup doesn't come gushing down and run all over the floor (and accidentally drown my hustler, I mean, date, who's passed out, drunk, on the floor). I freeze the runoff and use it for icing on cakes! The colors are so bright and vivid. Nothing says "Happy Birthday!" like Maybelline Blush #7.

I know what you're thinking: "Jeez, Bianca, isn't makeup toxic?" Honestly, I don't know. I've never had any complaints. Of course, I've never seen any of them ever again . . . Hmm . . .

Dear Bianca,

When you're having a bad day, what do you do to cheer yourself up?

Robert
Los Angeles

Robert,

That's easy: Dress up like a priest and fuck a kid.

Bianca:

I have a two-part question. 1. Do you believe in life after death? 2. What do you want your last words to be?

Jimmy

Boston, Massachusetts

Jimmy, Jimmy, Jimmy,

Two-part questions are actually two separate questions, and as I specifically noted on my website, people were asked to send in A question, not some questionS. So, unless you're schizophrenic or one half of a conjoined twin set, you've broken the rules. Yet, because I'm so good-natured and kind, I'll overlook your horrible fucking transgression and go on to answer your battery of questions.

But before I do, I must know, ARE you one half of a conjoined twin set? In which case, if I sleep with you, does it count as a three-way? When I was growing up we had conjoined twins living down the street from us. They were connected at the head. I remember the first time I saw them I asked my dear, sweet mother, "Mommy, are they boys or girls?" My mother lovingly replied, "What the fuck difference does it make? They're connected at the head!" The twins were quite lovely; hard to buy hats for, but lovely. And they had a great sense of humor. I'd call them a "two-faced bitch," and they'd laugh—out of both sides of their mouths. (FYI, back in the day, they were called "Siamese twins," because the first known pair, Chang and Eng, were born in Siam in 1811. I didn't know that until I did some research for this book. (And by *research* I mean I said to my longtime personal assistant, Jamie, "Hey, you in the leg irons, google 'freaks.'") Up until now I thought it was because the original conjoined twins were gay and knew the entire score of *The King and I*. Live and learn.)

Anyway, Jimmy, back to your questionSSS. 1. I have no idea if there's an afterlife, any more than I know if there's a heaven or a hell, or if there's a white person who eats at Popeye's. What I do know is that if there IS an afterlife, I pray it comes with water-resistant, hypoallergenic foundation and base. And 2. My last words will be "Not today, Satan."

Bianca,

My husband Jon wants to know how often you wash your belly button? He says he wants to know for science.

Lori
Flint, Michigan

Lori,

I saved the lint and made the blanket they filmed Lucy through in *Mame*.

Dear Bianca,

Where is your favorite place to fuck?

Curious Cathy
Midland, Texas

Cathy,

>Ask your husband. (FYI, your sheets need a higher thread count.)
>Still curious?

Dear Bianca,

>*What would you say if Donald Trump grabbed your pussy?*
>>*Nancy P*
>>*Washington, D.C.*

Nancy,

>I'd tell him to turn me over; you know he likes to flip properties.

Bianca:

>*If you were a tree, what kind of tree would you be?*
>>*Barbara W*
>>*New York City*

Babs,

>Have you seen *The Wizard of Oz*? I'd be that old, nasty tree. "Don't eat my apples!"

Dear Bianca,

>*How do you start your day?*
>>*Nikki*
>>*Miami Beach*

Nikki,

What is *day*? Whenever I ~~come to~~ wake up I have cereal . . . with vodka. Breakfast of champions!

———

Bianca,

Have you ever eaten food that came out of a Dumpster?
Amy
New York City

Dear Amy,

What kind of Dumpster, garbage or cum? Doesn't matter. Yes.

———

Dearest Bianca,

How can I convince my man to agree to adopt a puppy? I would love one. He is on the fence, afraid of the commitment.
Caring for a Canine
in Canada

Dear Caring,

If he's afraid of a commitment to a puppy, I'm guessing your man is never going to be a husband. If you're okay with that, and you REALLY want a puppy . . . promise him that you'll take complete and total care of the dog (feed, him, walk him, clean up the poop in the house) and he won't have to do anything. You'll be lying, of course, but so what? Besides, the dog will be temporary. You live in Canada; the poor thing will probably freeze to death before he's housebroken. (FYI, you're Canadian, I'm sure your government, and your very hot, very fuckable, very sane prime minister, have cheap prescription drugs available.)

Muah!

———————

Hey Bianca,

I am a commander of a national winning JROTC drill team down in southern Missouri. I am also a senior in high school and would love to hear back from you on how to handle stress at such a young age.

Alexis L

Dear Alexis,

I can't tell from your name if you're male or female. (I assume if you were transgender you would have causally mentioned it in your letter, like they all do. VERY annoying.) Alexis is one of those androgynous names, like Pat or Gene/Jean or Tilda Swinton. Regardless, I love that you're getting drilled in high school. How to handle stress? Easy—Drill, Baby, Drill! (If you're a boy, stop when you hit oil.)

———————

Dear Bianca:

What are your thoughts about the afterlife? What do you think happens when we die? I'm asking because I have severe anxiety about this topic. I know you don't know 100% what will happen, but I'm just curious to know what you think. Thank you!

Alina Khanbabaian ♥

Dear Sad Sack,

OMG! Congratulations!! You are the winner of the Dr. Kevorkian Most Depressing Person in the World Award. Your family will receive complimentary funeral services along with black veils, wilting flowers, and Kleenex! Alina, I have no idea how old you are, but unless you're ninety or hooked up to a breathing machine, you definitely need some counseling.

Afterlife? I can barely organize next Thursday. I have no idea what happens after we die. I think you should ask Shirley MacLaine. She's done it twenty-seven times. My guess is, if you're Catholic or Christian, you go to heaven or hell. If you're Buddhist, you go to another life. And if you're Jewish you go to Boca Raton. Your last name sounds Armenian, so I'm guessing you'll make a sex tape with a black man and then get a series on E!

As for me, if there is an afterlife, I hope to come back as a bench in the New York Yankees' locker room.

Hello Bianca,

I have a few questions to ask you.

First, what is the best way to break the ice with a guy you just met? I am so nervous in gay clubs and on gay dating websites and I always feel like I am going to make an idiot out of myself. How do you recommend I get over this?

Second, what is your Grindr profile? And what do you recommend as a funny bio for my profile? How about a quote from you? ;D

And thirdly, I am trying to complete my degree right now and I am losing all motivation to complete it. What words of advice would you give to me to keep going?

I spent four hours getting in drag for this. Why? If you think this picture is great, the next one is even better. The girl in the background walks into the wall.

I hope you get to answer these and I cannot wait to meet you in Dublin for Queens of Comedy!!

Love,
Dillon

Dear Dillon from Dublin,

How did you know that I LOVE alliterations! This Queen answers Questions Quickly! (Let's see Dear Fucking Abby do that!)

Easiest way to introduce yourself to a guy you just met is to take his dick out of your mouth, wipe off your chin, and say, "Hi, my name is Dillon!" Oh, wait—I just read the rest of the paragraph. You're talking about an actual DATE, which, I'm told, is when someone likes you and wants to get to know you. Since I've never been on one, can't help ya there, Princess. Sorry.

My Grindr profile is private, I've only given it out to 283,000 men. Again, sorry. But if you'd like a quote from me for your profile, how 'bout: "Dillon from Dublin has the Dick of Death!" ☺

As for your degree, I have no advice for you here, either. I make a living wearing gaudy makeup, fake tits, and nine-dollar wigs.

I feel bad that I didn't have great answers for all three of your questions, but then again, I asked people to send in ONE question, not three, so I don't feel that bad, you greedy fuck. You gays ruin everything.

Have a great day!
BDR

———

Bianca,

I have a tattoo of you on my arm. I've decided that I no longer want it since Bob was the better comedy winner. How do you recommend removing it?

Cassie W

Dear Cassie,

Cut your arm off. Cunt.

Muah ☺

———————————

Dear Miss B,

Every single day at my local supermarket there are various organizations asking for donations or selling things to raise money for Girl Scouts, Boy Scouts, VFW, anti-drug campaigns, pro-drug campaigns, children's hospitals, church groups, etc. You can't get in or out of the store without being accosted. I try to be charitable but it's starting to feel like an assault. Management says there's nothing they can do about it. Any suggestions?

Rita

Redondo Beach, California

Dear Rita,

Begging is sooooo fucking draining! I'm tired answering your question. I have a couple of thoughts. One, ALWAYS dress in black and wear a veil when you go shopping. Let them think you've lost your husband or a child. At some point they'll realize it's a scam and that it's not possible for you to have lost a loved one EVERY single week, or that you *have* lost someone every single week because you're a serial killer. Either way, they'll leave you alone. You can also wear a hazmat suit when heading to the market. No one will take money from an infectious loser.

And, Rita, if you're not afraid of confrontation, you could do what I do—march right up to them and say, "Charity begins at home. So go the fuck home!" (Note: This will not work if they're asking for money for the homeless.) Figure it out, Rita.

Dearest Bianca,

I don't know what to do with my hair. It's naturally wavy & frizzy, and when I try to straighten it, it becomes super oily. I can't stand the feel of most hair care products. What would you suggest I do?

Debbie S
Tempe, Arizona

Hi, Deb!

You don't say what race you are, but since you have oily, frizzy hair, I'm guessing it ain't white. Or Asian. ALL Asians have straight, wispy hair. Even their pubes are straight and wispy, like a cat's whiskers. I should know; I nearly poked my eyes out blowing the lead singer of the Japanese boy band One Dilection.

Short term, style your hair into one of those short, hip, rock-chick-like things, like Pink or Joan Jett, or Britney Spears, when she went through her "I'm mentally ill, please take my kids away" phase.

Long term, start chain-smoking. Eventually you'll get cancer and undergo chemotherapy, which will cause you to lose all your hair. Problem solved!

You're welcome.

P.S. Sometimes the hair grows back post-chemo, but it tends to stay short, so chins up!

MORE OF BIANCA'S PET PEEVES

FAT WOMEN AT COSTCO pushing wagons full of soda, chips, cookies, and pies. I'm dying to say, "Hey, Tubby! Give it a rest; there are skinny diabetics in Korea going to bed with low sugar levels tonight!"

WOMEN WITH SHOPPING CARTS overflowing with food who are on the checkout line at the supermarket for forty minutes, and wait until everything has been rung up to either pull out coupons or start writing a check. "Bitch, you were there for two-thirds of an hour. Why didn't you do this while you were waiting? I'm busy. I have places to go, things to do, people to blow!"

SIMILARLY, PEOPLE AT THE SUPERMARKET WHO HAVE ONE ITEM, let's say a pack of gum, and decide to write a check. If you can't come up with the ninety-nine cents for the gum you shouldn't be allowed to buy it.

OVERLY OFFICIOUS WAITERS AND WAITRESSES who come by the table every five minutes to see how I'm doing. I'm doing fine. If I'm not, I'll let you know, with a subtle gesture or a quick "Hey, apron-boy, get the fuck over here!"

SERVERS who use the expression *How is everything tasting?* "Well, the food is tasting fine, but the busboy's cock not so much."

WAITERS AND WAITRESSES WHO INSIST ON BEING CALLED "SERVERS." What's wrong with waiter or waitress? I don't insist on being called "bewigged and costumed comedic genius," do I? No. I'm perfectly fine with clapped-out old drag queen.

SALESPEOPLE WHO FOLLOW ME AROUND THE STORE, like the Nazi-hunter Jews who were looking for Adolf Eichmann. If I need your help, I'll find you. I'm trying out new mattresses; unless you plan on fucking me, I can do this alone. Besides, there are much better-looking salespeople than you. If I need help with this, I'll call one of them.

IMMIGRANTS WHO'VE BEEN IN THE COUNTRY FOR TEN YEARS AND STILL CAN'T SPEAK A WORD OF ENGLISH. In the course of a decade they should have accidentally learned a few simple words, like "Do you want me to trim the hedges, too?" or "Hey, mister, love you all night long, ten dollars," or "My back hurts from being chained in the hull of that boat for so long."

OLD PEOPLE WHO DRIVE IN FRONT OF ME, VERY SLOWLY, IN THE LEFT LANE ON THE FREEWAY. The left lane is for faster speeds; it's known as the passing lane. Keep it up, Grandpa, or it'll be known as the passing-away lane.

GUYS WHO DON'T WASH THEIR HANDS AFTER THEY PEE. Disgusting. And frightening—what if they want to put their fingers up my ass later that night? C'mon, that is totally not okay. Hygiene first!

WOMEN WHO WEAR WAY TOO MUCH PERFUME. I can't help but think it's to kill the smell from you know where. And I don't want to think about that, much less sniff the catch of the day.

MEN WHO WEAR WAY TOO MUCH COLOGNE. And by that I mean European or Russian men. I can't help but think it's to kill the smell from not bathing regularly.

PEOPLE WHO ARE ALWAYS FIVE MINUTES LATE FOR EVERYTHING. Once or twice, fine, shit happens—traffic was bad, you couldn't find your keys, the babysitter was late, whatever. But EVERY time? That's more than bad timing, it's passive-aggressive and hostile. And I've got a passive-aggressive, hostile remedy. I start every event half an hour before I tell these people it's scheduled. It's especially effective at weddings, funerals, last-rites ceremonies, and lottery drawings. You snooze, you lose. Sorry about it!

PEOPLE WHO CHECK THEIR CELL PHONES EVERY TWO MINUTES WHILE WE'RE HAVING DINNER. Unless you're an expectant father, a world leader, or a first responder, cut it the fuck out. I guarantee I'm way more interesting than whoever you think is going to text you. Unless the text is a sext from Brad Pitt, in which case, share it with me.

TOURISTS WHO WALK SLOWLY ON SIDEWALKS BECAUSE THEY'RE SIGHTSEEING, TAKING PICTURES, OR ASKING FOR DIRECTIONS. Here's an idea: Get a fucking map and move to the curb if you have to stop.

WOMEN WITH DUCK LIPS. Yes, I'm talking to you, Meg Ryan. Botox, yes. Filler, fine. Quack, quack, no. I don't get why these rich, middle-aged housewives need such thick puffy lips; it's not like they're going to give blow jobs or anything. (Present company excluded, and by present company I mean me.)

Miss Del Rio,

My boyfriend and I went to see your show recently and, while you were great (as always), we didn't have a very good time. The people a few rows in front of us stood for the entire show and we had trouble seeing you. They were asked to sit down, but refused. Any advice?

David
Chicago, Illinois

Dear David,

Buy better seats next time.

Muah!

Xoxo

Dear Bianca,

I'm 23 and gay. I want to move to a different city, or overseas. What are your favorite cities? And can you give the pros and cons of different cities I should consider?

Thank you!
Alan E
Houston, Texas

Dear Alan,

Starting a whole new chapter of your life is almost as exciting as unsnapping a Mormon boy's magic underpants while his parents are in the other room. There are a lot of great cities for you to consider, and I know them all like the back of my taint. But rather than answer your question in letter form, I'd rather make a list. For starters, you're the one moving, why should I be doing all the research? And second, in the time I save writing a quick list, I can get my nails done and my dick sucked. At the same time.

Dear Bianca,

　　Has Donald Trump ever grabbed your pussy? If he tried, would you let him? What should I do if he tries to grab mine?

Denny
Dover, Delaware

Dear Denny,

　　No.

　　No.

　　Say "no." Tell him you're holding out for Harvey Weinstein.

CITIES ALAN SHOULD CONSIDER MOVING TO

AMERICA

ASHEVILLE, NORTH CAROLINA
It's a great city, it just happens to be surrounded by North Carolina.

ATLANTA, GEORGIA
They used to call it Hotlanta. Then again, they used to call Madonna fuckable. Anyway, Atlanta can be fun as long as you're not there in the summer and don't mind the fact that everyone (including old ladies, toddlers, and maniacs) is carrying an assault weapon. It's also very confusing. Everything is named Peachtree. Even the mayor.

PORTLAND, OREGON
A little lezzie-infested, but if you don't mind hairy women with mannish hands, it's a very cool city. Progressive, smart, affordable, and lots of cruisy parks!

MIAMI, FLORIDA
Muy caliente! Great place to meet sexy young Cubans swimming in from Havana. Since they're illegal, *no habla ingles*, but they'll be happy to do whatever you ask. Even in bed. (I like to play *inmigración policía* and frightened houseboy.)

DENVER, COLORADO
Rocky Mountain High is right! Legal weed makes a good city a great city. Snowy in winter, gorgeous in summer, and just diverse enough to make it interesting without making it a melting pot. (FYI, the only melting pot I like is for fondue, which was a seventies thing like pet rocks, disco, and barebacking.) Definitely worth the schlep.

WASHINGTON, D.C.
Our nation's capital is a great place for a young man to make money—AND you don't have to be a lobbyist on K Street! There's a fortune to be had blackmailing Christian, Republican politicians after they've blown you in a public toilet. Plus, cherry blossom season is quite lovely.

AUSTIN, TEXAS
It's a great city, it just happens to be surrounded by Texas.

SEATTLE, WASHINGTON
Yes, it rains all the time, and yes, there are lots of serial killers.

BUT, the boys are smart, hip, and cute. And they're good in the sack because they can never go outside, so they're in bed all the time, "practicing."

BOSTON, MASSACHUSETTS
Fun for faaaaags. One side of the Chaaaaaales River is full of hot college students. The other side offers tough, straight, sexy Irish and Italian boys and Southies. If one of the straight, homophobic Southies beats you up after you blow him, one of the straight, "curious" Harvard Law students can file a lawsuit for you after you blow *him*. A win-win!

OCEANSIDE, CALIFORNIA
Five miles from Camp Pendleton. 'Nuff said.

NEW ORLEANS, LOUISIANA
My hometown, bitches! Any city that can produce *moi* is pretty fucking fabulous, *n'est-ce pas*? Cajun cock, delta dick, and bayou balls—and that's just my uncle. What's not to like?

NOT AMERICA

LONDON, UK

If you can handle the rain, the fog, the traffic, and the B.O., then London is for you. It's the gayest place on the planet because every single British man seems gay. The straightest guy in London is still pretty faggy. I don't know if it's the accents, the clothes, or the fact that they all love a Queen, but it's been my experience that the Brits are not only poofy, but horny and hung. Cheers!

PARIS, FRANCE

The French are smart, sexy, well dressed, cultured, racist, and anti-Semitic. On the downside, they all smoke. Paris is a toss-up. Oh, wait, Paris isn't racist and anti-Semitic. I was thinking of Alabama. My bad.

TEL AVIV, ISRAEL

A gay JEWbilee! Tel Aviv is a modern city in an ancient world. Lots of history, lots of spirituality, and lots of cut cock.

AMSTERDAM, THE NETHERLANDS

If it was good enough for Anne Frank, it's good enough for you. And because you have better taste and style, you'll probably have a better time. Have you ever seen her house? Total bore. But it's physically charming, so if you're even slightly more outdoorsy than Anne Frank, you'll be able to manage it just fine.

SYDNEY, AUSTRALIA

One part London, one part San Francisco, and one part New York, Sydney is fabulous. The Aussies spend 80 percent of their free time getting shitfaced at pubs and the other 20 percent getting tested at free clinics. Sydney is sexy and fun. You'll love Going Down. Under. G'day, bitch!

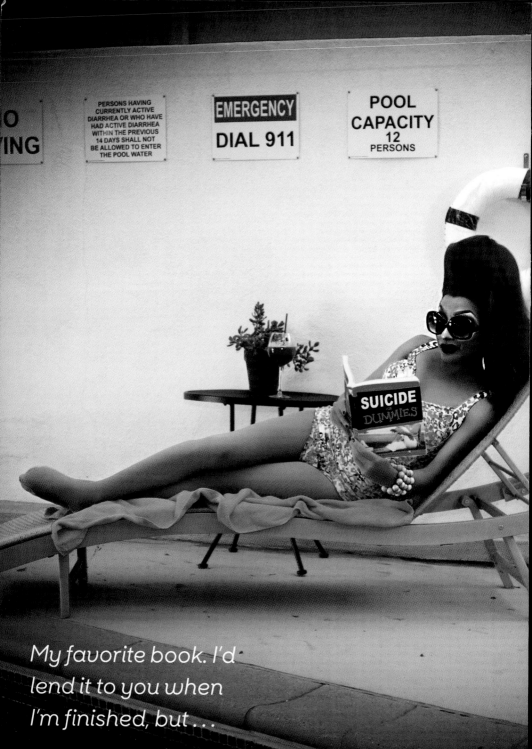

DISCLAIMER

Most authors put a disclaimer right in the front of the book so the people reading it know that it's a joke, written for laughs, and it's legally protected satire, so they won't get sued.

But I'm not most authors. I'm an author trying to get an endorsement deal with a giant pharmaceutical company. So if you read this book and your blood pressure rises, and you develop headaches or hives or arrhythmia, or an ulcer or Crohn's disease or gout—not only do I have zero liability for your condition, but I hope to make a lot of money finding a treatment.

You're welcome!

ABOUT THE AUTHOR

Drag queen. Comedian. Designer. Activist. Immigrant. Cunt.
BIANCA DEL RIO has been called many things, yet until now,
"author" was not one of them. But with *Blame It on Bianca Del Rio:
The Expert on Nothing with an Opinion on Everything*, the ultimate
advice manual, she becomes a published author, and her name
will be forever linked with such literary lions as Mark Twain, Ernest
Hemingway, Maya Angelou, and the homeless guy who wrote
"Suck My Dik, Fagit" on the walls of the 28th Street subway station in
New York.

Winning season six of *RuPaul's Drag Race* made Bianca the
cultural icon she is today. Prior to that she was best known as a
voice of reason, a dispensary of wisdom, a shoulder to cry on, and,
most important, the go-to gal for sage advice on all matters, big and
small.

"Discretion" is Bianca's middle name, which is why most people
don't know that she was indirectly responsible for some of the
world's most notable events. It was Bianca who advised Jackie
Kennedy to "wear something absorbent" in Dallas; it was Bianca
who told Michael Jackson that sleepovers were "tons of fun"; and
yes, it was Bianca who said to schoolteacher Christa McAuliffe, "Of
course you should go for a ride in the space shuttle; what's the worst
that could happen?"

Bianca felt that if her advice was good enough for them, it was
good enough for you, the public. Hence, *Blame It on Bianca Del*

Rio: The Expert on Nothing with an Opinion on Everything, the first volume in what will be, God/Allah/Buddha willing, a series of advice books (guides to life, really) from a man whose rise to international fame is based solely on duct tape, maxi pads, cheap vodka, and gaudy makeup.

The author lives in Los Angeles but tours the world extensively, and is known to ~~loiter~~ frequent truck stops, filling stations, and mini-marts in shady neighborhoods.